The Blue Stoops, Dronfield High Street (first building on the right), c1910 (Bob Gratton Collection).

North Derbyshire Pubs
Past and Present

Jim McIntosh

North Derbyshire Pubs Past and Present
Jim McIntosh

Published by
Pynot Publishing, 56 Main Road, Holmesfield, Dronfield, Derbyshire. S18 7WT
Tel & Fax: 0114 289 0348   Email: info@pynotpublishing.co.uk
Find us on the World Wide Web at www.pynotpublishing.co.uk

First Published 2008. Copyright 2008 © by Jim McIntosh.

Rights
All rights reserved. No part of this book may be reproduced or transmitted in any form or by any means, electronic or mechanical, including photocopying, recording, or by any information storage or retrieval system, without prior written consent from the publisher or author.

Printed and bound in the United Kingdom by Polestar-Wheatons, Exeter.

ISBN 978-0-9552251-6-1

If writing about pubs isn't a labour of love, I don't know what is? However, without the help of a number of people who shared information and photographs, I wouldn't have got this far.

In particular I would like to acknowledge assistance given to me by Alan & Ann Webster (Barley Mow, Bonsall), Albert Woodhead, Alun Waterhouse, Andy Bradley, Bernard Haigh, Bob Gratton, Prof. Brian Robinson, Dave Matthews, David Growns (formerly of the Rose & Crown, Barlborough), Doreen Buxton, Doug McIntosh (who took out all of the unnecessary brackets....apart from these), George Platts, Glynn Waite, John Chadwick, John Hassall, John Hirst, Ken Smith, Kevin Maidens (Blue Bell, Bolsover), Martyn Gillie (Arkwright Society), Maureen Lyon, Michael and Joyce Emmens, Ron Watson, Nick Williams, Sandra Ballantyne, Stewart Wood and Trevor Nurse.

Thanks are also due to Nick Wheat (layout, essential publishing expertise and cups of coffee), Helen Frances (for the fantastic illustrations and Dronfield map), Lulu Landale (proof reading and should there be a comma here, or not?) and the staff at Chesterfield Local Studies Library, Dronfield Library and Sheffield Local Studies Library. Nearer to home, I am grateful to Gill for her support and Eleanor for being great company when her dad is taking her out to visit yet another pub. Can't wait for the day that you learn to drive!

The pub is an integral part of this country's social history and fabric. If ignored they can be turned into a house as quick as the Planning Team at the local council can say 'approved'. So whilst reading this, why don't you make plans to visit some of the pubs that are mentioned?

Cheers!

Jim McIntosh
April 2008
Barlborough, Derbyshire

CONTENTS

Apperknowle	4
Barlborough	6
Baslow (Robin Hood)	11
Birchinlee (Derwent Canteen)	11
Birchover (Red Lion)	13
Bolsover	14
Bonsall	18
Brimington	20
Coal Aston	24
Cromford (including part of Wirksworth)	25
Dronfield	30
Dronfield Woodhouse	36
Eckington (lost pubs)	36
Elmton (Elm Tree)	38
Handley	38
Higham	40
Holmesfield	42
Marsh Lane	43
New Whittington	45
Old Whittington	47
Ridgeway (part)	49
Sutton Cum Duckmanton	49
Taddington	51
Troway	53
Unstone	55
Whitwell	56
Have they always been known as pubs?	59
Closed Pubs	60
Bibliography	61

APPERKNOWLE

The first reference to a settlement at Apperknowle was made in 1317 and it has also been known as Apelknol, Hapilknole and Appurknoll. The common local theory behind the name is that it originates from 'apple tree on the knoll', i.e. small hill, but whilst this is disputed by Cameron in 'Place Names of Derbyshire', he does not offer an alternative suggestion. The makeup and population of the area altered after Apperknowle colliery was sunk in the 1840s. The colliery was purchased by the Unstone Company in the latter part of the 19th century and was located towards the top of the ridge off Moortop Road; an iron shelter stands on the approximate site today. For further information on this and other North East Derbyshire collieries, there is an excellent web resource run by A.N. Bridgewater: http://myweb.tiscali.co.uk/colliery.

Alehouse and un-named beerhouses

There were no drinking establishments in Apperknowle until the 1840s. The earliest known alehouse in the area was on Crow Lane, down the hill towards Unstone. The property is still standing and is now known as Siscar Cottage; Michael Gill and William Gill held victuallers licences during the periods 1754-1774 and 1797-1819 respectively.

The first evidence of a licensed premise actually at Apperknowle was an un-named beerhouse operated by a Thomas Wright, who was also a farmer, which was listed in Trade Directories for 1846 and 1857. However the beerhouse is not mentioned in census records for that period and it is not known if this was a forerunner of one of the named pubs below. Two further beerhouses were recorded in an 1895 Trade Directory; one was operated by Francis Reed, who was also a butcher, the other by William Sheppard. Nothing else is known about either of these businesses.

Barrack Hotel   Barrack Road

Built in 1852, the Barrack Hotel may be found at Town End, which is the oldest part of Apperknowle. The original beerhouse only occupied part of the current premises and a butcher's shop occupied the Summerley end. The Barrack Hotel was first recorded in the 1871 census and was restricted to selling beer only until a full licence was obtained in 1949. Major alterations to the pub were undertaken in 1987 although part of the original bar façade was retained.

Known owners include Chater & Co., who paid £950 in April 1883, and Brampton Brewery of Chesterfield. The current owners, John & Rachel Eggleston, bought the pub in the 1990s and have developed a reputation for the quality of their real ale that saw them receive Chesterfield CAMRA's Spring Pub of the Season award in 2006.

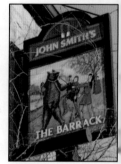

Signboard from the 1990s.
[Brian Curtis/Inn Sign Society]

Whilst a barrack normally refers to a building for lodging soldiers, the pub's name is a reference to the practice of bear baiting that is said to have taken place nearby and therefore barrack is being used in the sense of shouting or jeering. Indeed the pub's signboard in the 1990s (pictured) showed two youths teasing a tethered bear.

Miner's Arms   Hundall Lane

Located at the nearby hamlet of Hundall, this was originally a farmhouse/homestead belonging to the Stephenson family. A beerhouse was opened sometime after the property was sold in 1858; a fact confirmed by the 1871 census, when the licensee was Joseph Breedon, who was also a coal miner. Previous owners include two breweries: Thomas Berry of Sheffield and then Tennant Brothers, via their takeover of the former in August 1924. The beerhouse licence was converted to a full licence in the early 1950s and the pub remains a traditional community local.

Royal Oak — *Summerley Road*

This beerhouse used to be found just beyond Apperknowle at Summerley, on the road to Coal Aston, and was built as a cottage in the 1840s. The first evidence that it was operating as a beerhouse comes in the 1871 census when occupied by Henry Hardwick, another coal miner. The beer was supplied by Scarsdale Brewery and there were no beer pumps; instead beer was served by jug direct from the cellar. The last landlord, Jack Easterbrook, was known to all as 'Mad Jack' and there are many stories of his antics, as documented in Sheffield CAMRA's 'Beer Matters' magazine. The pub closed in the 1960s when he was no longer able to pay his debts and is now a private dwelling, 'Oak Cottage'. In a sale particulars document from the latter part of the 20th century, it was described as having an inner reception hall with built in bar/servery with Formica top, no doubt a remnant from its days as a pub.

Travellers' Rest — *High Street*

Originally a beerhouse, its first mention is in the 1871 Census, when the licensee was John Hill, aged 58 years. Whilst it has not been possible to establish an accurate opening date, it is known that Scarsdale Brewery held the lease for the pub in the early 1900s. Known as the Reference Point for a brief period in the late 1980/early 1990s, the Traveller's remains a popular and busy pub as at 2007.

Yellow Lion — *High Street*

Yellow Lion in 2001. [Roy Shorrock]

The 1861 Census lists Godfrey Ward, a Scale Presser and Innkeeper aged 44, at 'The Yellow Lion Inn', although legal documents suggest that the current building dates from 1864/5. Godfrey Ward sold the Yellow Lion in 1876 for £1300, plus fixtures, to William Harrison and George Howe, respectively a Brewery Manager and Brewery Clerk of Highfields, Sheffield. In 1901 the pub was bought by Sheffield brewers Whitmarsh, Watson & Co., whose brewery and pubs were bought by Duncan Gilmour and Co. in 1906. Gilmours themselves fell to Tetleys in 1954. Michael (Mick) Emmens became licensee in 1969 when the pub was still tied to Tetleys, buying the freehold in 1986. Mick and his wife, Joyce, ran the pub until it closed on 7th September 2003. The premises are now a private house. The original entrance was on the west side, facing the Post Office and it is probable that this was moved to the front in the early 1900s when Gilmour & Co. became owners.

BARLBOROUGH

Barlborough, meaning 'boar' or 'barley clearing', is one of the most historic villages in North East Derbyshire and is mentioned in the Domesday Book. During the 19th century the population of Barlborough nearly trebled on the back of an expansion in coal mining in the area, also leading to an increase in the number of public houses and beerhouses.

Apollo   High Street

The Apollo was first listed in an 1833 Trade Directory when John Pattinson was both the licensee and parish clerk. It is thought to have been the first commercial hotel in Barlborough and indeed was referred to as the 'Apollo Inn' in Trade Directories from 1879 onwards, indicating that lodgings for travellers were available, as well as alcoholic refreshment.

The premises, thought to have been built in the 1700s by the Staniforth family, were severely damaged by a fire which occurred in the early morning of 20th March 1930. The licensee, Mrs Katie Keel, was returning from a night out at the Bolsover Police Ball, at around 3.45am, when she "perceived a strong smell of fire" and found that the flames had reached the roof. Whilst most parts of the pub were severely damaged, it was still possible to serve customers from the clubroom whilst reconstruction took place. Katie Keel was later licensee of the Rose & Crown in Barlborough and her daughter, Ellen ('Nellie') Bower, was licensee of the Royal Oak, also in Barlborough.

Drinkers at the Apollo were able to enjoy beers from Wards Brewery of Sheffield, during the period 1990-1999, until Wards pubs were sold off to the Pubmaster chain and Wards Brewery closed. This followed a decision by the accountants at the parent company, Swallow Hotel Group, to close two profitable breweries, Vaux at Sunderland was also closed, in a move regarded as unnecessary by many observers. The pub is now operated by the Punch Taverns Pub Company.

Blacksmiths' Arms   Sheffield Road (Low Common)

First listed as early as 1841 when a Joseph Haigh ran a beerhouse at Low Common. Haigh continued there until the 1850s and as he was also listed as a blacksmith, it is likely that this beerhouse was the Blacksmiths' Arms. During this period the premises were modernised in 1855. The next licensee, John Swift, was also a blacksmith and was first listed in an 1860 Trade Directory.

In the 20th century the Blacksmiths' Arms was owned by Barlborough Hall Estate, Scarsdale Brewery (Chesterfield) and Sheffield Free Brewery. Subsequently it was bought by William Stones Ltd. It is now owned by Century Inns.

The pub is known locally as the 'Sprag', a miner's term, and a reference to props used in the early 1900s to support the edge of the road which passes very close to the front of the pub. The road in question, which is now a busy route linking Eckington with Barlborough and the M1 motorway, stands well above the level of the pub and at one time was thought to be in danger of collapsing onto the 'Sprag'.

Crown & Anchor   West End

Situated at West End (across the road from the old Barlborough water tower), the Crown & Anchor existed as a beerhouse and subsequently a fully licensed public house for just over 60 years. It was first recorded under that name in 1862 when run by Samuel Woodhead, a 60-year old lime burner. By 1868 the Crown & Anchor had a full licence and records also show that it was later owned by Wards of Sheffield. It closed in May 1923 when the licence expired; the premises were demolished in the 1930s. The premises are remembered as being built of brick, with brown and green glazed-tiles around its entrance. As Samuel Woodhead is also known to have been a brick and tile maker, he may even have built his beerhouse.

Dusty Miller   *Sheffield Road*

The original Dusty Miller in the 1890s. [Andy Bradley collection]

First listed in 1862 when the landlord was Thomas White. The Dusty Miller was originally situated in one of the stone cottages that stand close by before it moved to its current location in the 1930s. By the 1920s it was owned by Truswells Brewery, Sheffield, which was taken-over by Hope & Anchor Breweries, also of Sheffield, in 1955. It is now a privately owned freehouse and hosts regular live music nights.

Horns Inn   *Church Street/Worksop Road*

The Horns Inn is first mentioned, along with the Rose & Crown, in Fairbank's General Survey of Barlborough, which was undertaken in 1798 and published in 1805. Old maps show that it had its own stables and yard, and there was also a maltings and brewhouse at the rear of the premises, not uncommon at that time. The name is a reference to the fact that a major source of business was from the stagecoaches that passed through Barlborough on their journey between Chesterfield and Worksop. The post-horn would be sounded to warn a landlord of the imminent arrival of the next coach.

By 1830/1 the Horns Inn seems to have been incorporated into the newly built Rodes' Arms, later known as the De Rodes Arms (see below), and the premises were converted into its clubroom. Unfortunately this piece of Barlborough's history was lost when the De Rodes clubroom was destroyed by a fire which occurred on 12th October 1926.

Miners Arms   *High Street*

A beerhouse, the Miners Arms was first listed in 1895, when Rachel Talbot was licensee. It was a stone building and situated to the rear and right hand side of the Apollo, set back about 50 yards from the road. Until 1908 it was owned by Scarsdale Brewery, Chesterfield, before being bought by Ind Coope. This beerhouse then became a casualty of the 1904 Licensing Act, 'The Compensation Act', which allowed local magistrates to close licensed premises, in return for a compensation payment, in areas where they felt there were too many. The Miners Arms closed on 15th December 1910 and following closure, the premises were converted into two cottages (now demolished).

Pebley Inn   Rotherham Road

A 1950s view of the Pebley Inn.

An old coaching inn built around 1770, the Pebley Inn stands on the ancient Sheffield-Newark-London turnpike road and falls in the county of Derbyshire by only a few hundred yards. Evidence of a blacksmith's shop and stone steps for mounting horses used to be visible and there were stables on the left hand side of the pub. There was also a sleeping area for the ostlers, stable lads who worked at the inn, which contained a large bed where up to 12 could sleep at one time.

The Pebley has been owned by two noted local families: De Rodes in the 19th century and Sitwells in the 20th. Sir Osbert Sitwell sold the Pebley to William Stones Ltd in 1947 and it then passed to Bass in 1970 before regaining freehouse status in 1991 when purchased by Liz and Ian Bell. As at 2007 it is a popular pub with a range of well kept real ales, including some from local independent breweries and is owned and run by Chris & Andrea Dennis.

The source of the pub's name is from the ancient name for the area in which it stands, one mile to the north east of Barlborough. It was first referred to a Pybbelay, Pybba's clearing, in the thirteenth century, and later Pubbelay. The latter may have been derived from Egidius de Publey, who was of Norman descent and lived nearby.

Prince of Wales   Sheffield Road (Low Common)

The Prince of Wales was built in 1864 as a beerhouse by local mine owner and entrepreneur Miles Barber. It was part of a small community, named 'Barbers Row', which he developed to provide housing and amenities for miners working at his colliery. The 40 or so cottages that comprised Barbers Row have long since disappeared but the pub remains.

The Prince of Wales was originally a beerhouse and the sizeable premises have also doubled as a commercial hotel and for many years a shop was situated next to the pub. Previous owners include Tennant's Brewery and etched windows still evidence this fact. The pub is now back in private hands and operates as a hotel, although the restaurant and bar are also open to the public.

Rodes' Arms/De Rodes' Arms   Worksop Road

The Rodes' Arms was first mentioned in 1830/1 by John Thomas in 'Walks in the neighbourhood of Sheffield'. It was originally known as the Rodes' Arms, the 'De' not being introduced until the 1860s by W Hatfield De Rodes. The Rodes/De Rodes family have played an important part in Barlborough life for nearly 500 years and a family member, Francis Rodes, was one of the judges who tried Mary Queen of Scots.

The pub has an ideal location next to where two ancient toll roads cross and in 1831 also acted as the post office. In 1835 a coach, 'Champion', ran twice weekly from outside the pub to Sheffield.

Police attend the murder and suicide scene in March 1907. [Andy Bradley collection]

In March 1907, the De Rodes made the news for all the wrong reasons. "Publican murders bailiff" was the headline in the 'Derbyshire Times', which went on to report that: "Miles Gosling, landlord of the De Rodes Arms, kills William Mullinger before committing suicide". Mullinger was a bailiff who was attempting to collect a debt of £60 on behalf of the brewery.

Records show that in 1953 the pub was owned by the De Rodes family and leased to Worksop & Retford Brewery. A clock evidencing this link to the brewery could still be found in the pub in the 1990s. Worksop & Retford were acquired by Tennant Brothers of Sheffield in 1959, and Tennants themselves subsequently merged with Whitbread in 1961-2. The pub was one of 239 Whitbread pub restaurants bought by Mitchell & Butlers PLC in 2006, for an equivalent £2.1m per site, and now operates under the 'Innkeepers Fayre' brand with a focus on family eating.

Rose & Crown   High Street

The Rose & Crown pictured in 1910. [Andy Bradley collection]

The oldest pub in Barlborough, it is said to have stood in the same position for more than three hundred years. Its prime position next to the historic cross, thought to have Norman origins, suggests it is one of the oldest buildings in that part of the village.

Barlborough is not mentioned in Sir Francis Leek's 'Survey of Alehouses, Innes and Tavernes in the County of Derby', undertaken in 1577, and instead the earliest evidence of the Rose & Crown is in the 'Dickenson Survey' of 1723, when it was the only inn listed in Barlborough. Licensing records show that the landlord during the period 1777-1800 was a Robert Webster, who was pictured with the pub in a drawing 'Wakes at Barlborough Cross' dated 1785 by the Swiss artist S H Grimm.

A fish and chip shop once stood next to the pub but this was demolished in the 1970s and the land used for the Rose & Crown restaurant extension.

In the 20th century the pub was owned by the Barlborough Hall Estate, which also owned the Royal Oak, and the Blacksmiths Arms in Barlborough, and it was later a William Stones's house. In 1991 it was part of a package of 36 pubs in North East Derbyshire sold to Hardys & Hansons PLC for £6.5m. A further change of ownership came in 2006 when Greene King bought the Hardys & Hansons brewery and its estate of pubs. Unfortunately this means you can no longer enjoy a pint of Kimberley, although the ubiquitous Greene King IPA is available. It is however difficult to surpass the enjoyment from supping a well-kept pint in the pub's beer garden on a summer's evening.

Royal Oak   High Street

Whilst the building was erected by the Rodes family in 1724, it was not used as licensed premises until 1863 or 1864. This coincided with the closure of the Clock Wheel and possibly the licence was transferred to the Royal Oak. The first landlord, George H Pattinson, was also a farmer. For many years the pub was owned by the Barlborough Hall Estate, being leased to Stones's Brewery in 1953. A profile of the pub in the 'Sheffield Spectator' in October 1965 revealed that the then landlady, Mrs Ellen ('Nellie') Bower, had been at the pub since 1945. As an aside, Nellie Bower's husband, Walter ('Cocky') Bower, patented the 'Bower Wheel', a cast-iron wheel manufactured locally at Renishaw Foundry. The wheels were attached to tractors to assist when working on heavy clay soils.

The local hunt outside the Royal Oak in 1955. [Andy Bradley collection]

Standing across the road from the Apollo in the centre of the village, the Royal Oak is a popular pub with a busy restaurant area.

Treble Bob   Midland Way

The first new pub in Barlborough for over 100 years, the Treble Bob opened in 1998 at Barlborough Links. The name was derived from a bell-ringing method used at Barlborough St. James Church in 1928 to commemorate the coming of age of Miss Stella Locker-Lampson, the daughter of Godfrey Locker-Lampson M.P., the last private owner of Barlborough Hall. The pub is a Tom Cobleigh 'purpose built family pub' and has a children's play barn, ultimate owners being the Spirit Group.

Wheel/Clock Wheel   *Church Street/Twychell*

Licensed Victualler records show that since 1787 William Milner, who was also a blacksmith, had held a licence for an alehouse in Barlborough. It is thought that this was the 'Wheel', as listed in an 1821/2 Directory when a Mary Milner was licensee. It was referred to as the 'Clock Wheel' in an 1833 Trade Directory (although confusingly it reverted back to the 'Wheel' in an 1835 Directory) and was situated on 'Twychell' at the centre of the village, close to the well and near the church. The premises were said to have been timber-framed, with a thatched roof. It is also known that the last licensee, William Whitworth, was also a blacksmith.

It is said that the Clock Wheel was forced to close after the premises were destroyed by fire during the period 1862/3, consistent with an 1864 directory entry which shows that whilst Whitworth was still working as a blacksmith, the Clock Wheel was no longer listed.

The pub's unusual name is mentioned in 'English Inn Signs' (Larwood and Hotten, 1866, revised and reprinted in 1985) where the derivation of the name is attributed to a corruption of 'Catherine Wheel', once a common inn sign. However an alternative theory is that the name 'Wheel' reflected the fact that refreshment was available for stagecoaches passengers and the 'Clock' prefix was added later to acknowledge its close proximity to the church clock, which would have been visible from the premises.

BASLOW

Robin Hood   *Chesterfield Road*

Situated at 'Robin Hood', according to Ordnance Survey (OS) maps, which gives rise to the question of 'which came first - the name or the pub?' According to Cameron, in 'Place Names of Derbyshire', the place name is derived from the inn, and he quotes the source for this as an OS map in 1840. Further confirmation comes by way of anecdotal evidence that there has been an inn near to Birchen Edge since the 1700s. The land and buildings belonged to the Duke of Rutland until 1920, when the pub was sold to Chesterfield Brewery. The property was rebuilt in the 1960s, whilst owned by Mansfield Brewery, and a first floor added and, following further brewery takeovers/mergers/name changes, it is now part of Marston's.

BIRCHINLEE

Derwent Canteen

Now largely forgotten and with little evidence of its existence remaining, the Derwent Canteen, constructed of corrugated iron, had existed for around 15 years in a temporary settlement near Bamford.

Parliamentary approval for the Derwent & Howden dams' project included provision of workers' housing, reflecting longstanding concerns about the living conditions of 'navvies' on major construction projects. When the nearby Woodhead railway tunnel was constructed in the 1840s, one parliamentary observer likened the scale of deaths and injuries from accidents and disease to "the results of a small battle". To accommodate the work force, the Derwent Valley Water Board (DVWB) constructed a purpose-built settlement at Birchinlee. The village stood 800 feet above sea level and took the name of 'Birchinlee' from an old farmhouse that formerly stood at its northern end.

Known locally as 'Tin Town', because the buildings were constructed of corrugated iron, the settlement housed between 250 and 500 people between 1901 and 1914 whilst the Derwent and Howden dams were completed. The best known dam in the valley, Ladybower, was built between 1935 & 1945.

Pulling a beer in the canteen. [Prof. Brian Robinson collection]

Housing comprised dormitories for single men, smaller huts for married men with families and separate huts for foremen, all arranged in formal rows separated by track ways. Facilities included two hospitals, a school and mission room, Post Office, greengrocers, cobbler and hairdresser, clothier and draper, confectioner and tobacconist, bath-house, a recreation hall and police station. Of specific interest here was the 'Derwent Canteen', which was licensed to sell beer.

The Works Committee sanctioned the canteen in June 1901 and a provisional licence was granted at the annual licensing meeting at Chapel-en-le-Frith in September 1901 on the understanding that the licence would only exist during the period of the building of the dams. The canteen opened for business on 30th November 1901 and records show that its fixtures, beer engine and counter were valued at £110 for insurance purposes.

Management of the canteen was undertaken by the People's Refreshment House Association (PRHA) for an initial management fee of £75 per annum and the known managers/licensees of the canteen were:

Arnut Pack	Nov 1901 - Mar 1902
Arthur Manning	Mar 1902 - May 1903
Henry Matthews	May 1903 - July 1907
Mr Mitchell	Dates not known

One question that needs answering is were the DVWB looking to set up a model establishment to meet the social needs of their workers, or given that navvies always drank, often to excess, did they just want to ensure that the resulting profits did not end up elsewhere? Before the canteen opened they had made the right noises - the licence application had stated that the 'model' house would prevent the men going off to the nearest inn at Ashopton, getting drunk there, and becoming a nuisance upon their return.

However, the Works Committee's true objectives emerged during a dispute with temperance campaigners. A representative from the Temperance Society visited Birchinlee, subsequently writing: "The canteen is just the same as any other pub. We see lots of men reeling about drunk.

You should see them at night". He also reported that even the village PC was seen drinking in the bar! It was further alleged that the first licensee, Arnut Pack, had tried to limit workers' beer consumption and had been driven out for his trouble.

The Works Committee investigated Temperance Society allegations of drunkenness, discussed the matter....and decided to enlarge the canteen to overcome issues of overcrowding, as identified by the temperance campaigners. Overall, the efforts of the temperance movement to discredit the canteen were in vain. Indeed the canteen was subsequently extended again on several occasions. This included an additional room built in 1906 for use by customers not requiring alcoholic drinks – the only success for the temperance campaigners.

The canteen was a profitable venture, with annual profits during the period 1903-14 often exceeding £2000 and the DVWB only returned small sums to the villagers, for example £20 in March 1903 for a concert at the recreation hall. Canteen profits also funded books for the village library and the ceremony to celebrate the completion of the Howden Dam in September 1912.

Evidence that the DVWB wanted to ensure that only they made profits from the drinking needs of their workforce comes from the tough stance they took against all possible competition to the Derwent Canteen. Firstly, they bought the Ashopton Inn from the Duke of Devonshire in 1902. Although it was eight miles away at Ashopton, this was the nearest pub to Birchinlee. The PRHA took over management of the inn in January 1905.

To ensure that their monopoly was not infringed, DVWB took steps to block any licence applications that would create competition. For example, in 1901 a Mr Pickford proposed to apply for a licence for a canteen to be called the 'Crook Hill Canteen'. Conveniently for the DVWB, the application was withdrawn. It is not known what pressure the DVWB exerted to achieve this outcome. Finally, DVWB opposed an application, made by a Mr A Muir Wilson on behalf of Mr. J A Wilson, for a canteen to serve the Bamford and Howden railway project, then in the course of construction.

Unfortunately it has not been possible, to date, to establish which brewery supplied the canteen with beer. There was no facility for brewing beer on site and instead beer would have been delivered to the canteen by the railway, the prime use of which was to take construction materials up to the dam.

On completion of the dams' construction, the canteen building was sold to an unknown purchaser in September 1915 as part of the dismantling of the village. Its fate is unknown. An archaeological survey in the early 1990s discovered a 3 metre deep stone-lined hollow with a doorway - part of the canteen's beer cellar. Still in situ today, this is the sole evidence of its existence.

BIRCHOVER

Red Lion *Barton Hill*

The history of this pub begins when the current premises were built in 1680 on the site of a farmstead. By 1722 the premises were licensed, and known as the 'Red Lion' whilst the landlord for the period 1822-46 was George Gregory junior. Looking at the wider area, there were three licensed victuallers recorded in the area in licensing records for 1753. As well as the Red Lion, the other two are believed to have been the Flying Childers (Stanton in Peak) and the Thorn Tree, also at Birchover. Little information has come to light about the latter although it may have been located on Winster Road in a building now occupied by Uppertown farm (known to have been licensed premises at the some stage).

BOLSOVER

The derivation of the name 'Bolsover' is a matter of dispute, so we need to swot up on our etymology before we can tackle the more basic pleasures of beer and pubs. In the late 19th century, the Rev E. Andrews Downman proposed that the name 'Bolsover' was derived from a heathen god called 'Bel', and appropriately means 'Bel's high place'. Alternative explanations are both more mundane, and more likely. One suggestion is that it means 'a place near bullock pasture', although Cameron, in 'Derbyshire Place Names' (1959), dismisses this as "far from convincing". Instead, his preferred explanation is that the name comes from an Anglo-Saxon landowner, long since forgotten, called either Bul or Bol. The second part of the name, 'over' (or ovre), refers to a slope. Putting all this together gives us the meaning of Bul's (or Bol's) slope. As we can never know for certain, it must be time to move on.

13th century Bolsover was a thriving town with a market and castle and was probably at least equal in importance to Chesterfield. At the beginning of industrialisation, the town's craftsmen specialised in buckles, spurs and clay pipes. However, the arrival of 'King Coal' in the last quarter of the 19th century had much more impact and brought people, jobs and money to the area. Now of course, nearly all of the coal-related activities have gone.

Before we look at the pubs and beerhouses that are known to have existed, here are a few notes on the main breweries that we will come across. A number of Bolsover pubs originally belonged to Chesterfield Brewery. In 1935 the assets of Chesterfield Brewery, including its pubs, were purchased by Mansfield Brewery, which in 1999 was purchased by Wolverhampton & Dudley (W&D). In 2007 W&D renamed itself after its best known brand – Marston's. Rather than repeat this tale numerous times, pubs will be referred to as 'ex-Chesterfield brewery', unless they are no longer owned by Marston's.

The Anchor Inn c.1910 [Dave Matthews collection]

Anchor Inn   Market Place
The Anchor is a former Brampton Brewery pub and was already open when the first trade directory covering Bolsover was produced in 1821/2. Formerly a Wards pub, it is now owned by Pubmaster.

Angel   Castle Street
The Angel, situated near Bolsover castle, was originally an old coaching inn constructed of stone with metal casement windows and a red pantiled roof. It is said that it was in the hands of the Adsetts family for 300 years and that travellers visiting Bolsover and the castle would have used the inn. The old building has, however, been replaced by the present one and the pub is now owned by Enterprise Inns.

Appletree Inn   Clowne Road
Situated at Stanfree, the Appletree Inn was originally a beerhouse owned by Scarsdale Brewery. Whilst the year of opening is not known, this must have been by 1870 as beerhouse licences were generally not issued after that. The pub was saved from closure in 1997 when Bolsover District Council won their appeal against conversion to a residential nursing home.

Barley Mow (aka Old Thatch) *Hill Top*

The Barley Mow, known locally as the 'Old Thatch' or Thatched House Tavern, stood at Hill Top. The original building had a thatched roof, which gave the pub its nickname. Licensing records show that this was a beerhouse owned or leased by Chesterfield Brewery until the pub closed in 1904, and its licence passed to the Carr Vale Hotel. The building was subsequently demolished and the site is now occupied by the Assembly Hall car park. The Carr Vale Hotel (Chesterfield Brewery) subsequently closed and is now a supermarket.

Black Bull *Hill Top*

Chesterfield Brewery bought the Black Bull for the princely sum of £860 in June 1884 from Mr Cree. Mansfield Brewery subsequently sold the pub to Burtonwood Brewery in April 1989. The pub was also known as the Bull & Dog until the late 1830s.

Blue Bell *High Street*

Helen Frances

Whilst the current Blue Bell premises were built in 1749, it is thought that another inn previously stood on the site. Given its proximity to the church, this seems plausible; names incorporating 'Bell' were commonly given to hostelries near churches to attract business from travellers, many on horseback, visiting the church. Indeed at the rear there is still evidence of stables and a manger. The interior of the pub has been altered considerably, for the original living accommodation for the licensee and his family was downstairs with the upstairs rooms being available for use by guests. In the 1920s, a car hire business was also advertised as operating from the pub. Ex-Chesterfield Brewery, the pub is a traditional local with a warm welcome and four good quality real ales and, in recognition of these attributes, was voted the Chesterfield CAMRA 'Pub of the Year' for 2007. There are some great views from the beer garden.

A charabanc excursion pictured outside the Blue Bell in the 1920s. [Dave Matthews collection]

Castle Arms   Station Road
The Castle Arms is a 20th century pub situated within sight of Bolsover castle. Approval was given in 1953 for Mansfield Brewery to build this new pub, with the licence being transferred from the Nags Head. Plans, by J.B. Cutts, were approved in 1954, estimated cost of pub £25,000. It opened on Monday 22nd December 1958. It is now a Marston's pub and has an outdoor children's play area.

Cavendish Hotel   Market Place
The source of the Cavendish name is from the family name of the Duke of Devonshire. It was originally called the Vaults until 1886, and is ex-Chesterfield Brewery.

Cross Keys   Market Place
The Cross Keys can be found right in the town centre. It is believed that it was rebuilt in the early 20th century. It was once a Home Brewery pub.

Cross Keys pictured in 1911. [Dave Matthews collection]

Fidlers Rest   Craggs Road
The property which is now the pub was originally built as a house in 1812 by local man, Peter Fidler, and named 'Hudson Bay House'. Around 1856, a Joseph Fidler turned it into a Public House and named it the Hudson Bay Beerhouse. Between 1889 and 1900 the name was changed to the Castle Inn and it then alternated between the Castle and Hudson during the 20th century. In September 2002, following a sympathetic refurbishment which successfully incorporates the old well in the floor of the bar, the pub re-opened with its original name, but in 2007 this was changed to Fidlers Rest.

The Hudson Bay and Fidlers Rest names recall that Peter Fidler worked as a surveyor for the famous Hudson Bay Company in Canada. In November 1792 Fidler journeyed from Canada's most westerly post, Buckingham House on the North Saskatchewan River. On his way south-westward from the parklands across the plains, Fidler made a number of valuable observations about the way of life of the nomadic buffalo hunting peoples he encountered. He was also the first European to explore and write about Southern Alberta. Fidler built the property that is now the pub in 1812 as a home for his mother during a visit to his home town. He never lived in the property himself as he spent the rest of his life in Fort Dauphin, Western Canada.

King of Hearts — *Moorfield Avenue*

The King of Hearts opened on 4th February 1956 but survived less than forty years. Situated on Moorfield Avenue, it was subsequently known as Cromwells before closing in May 1994. At one stage Shipstones Brewery (Nottingham) were owners.

Nags Head — *Station Road*

Nags Head prior to closure. [John Hirst collection]

Originally called the Barley Mow until about 1860 when it was rebuilt, it is thought that the pub may originally have been created out of two or more terraced properties. Chesterfield Brewery bought the pub around 1882 and it was eventually closed by Mansfield Brewery to enable them to transfer the licence to a new pub, the Castle Arms (see earlier). On the licence application, it was stated that a licence had been in existence for 200 years. The pub closed prior to the opening of the Castle Arms on 22 December 1958. The premises, now demolished, were situated on the opposite side of the road to the Castle Arms and further up the hill towards Bolsover (an area known as Hockley).

Quiet Woman — *Houfton Road*

A new pub which opened on 21st July 1962. Originally Hammonds United Breweries were owners but the Quiet Woman is now a free house.

Royal Oak — *Stanfree*

Records show that this pub at Stanfree has been in existence since 1776. Francis Shacklock, the licensee in 1857, must have been multi-talented as he was also a clockmaker. The pub was closed after an application to renew the licence was refused in 1870. The unlucky owner was a Mr Williamson of the Albert Inn, Staveley.

Sportsman — *Villas Road*

The Sportsman was built around 1896 by the Bolsover Colliery Company Ltd in New Bolsover 'Model Village' as a village institute to provide meeting and reading facilities. Whilst the institute did offer alcohol, miners were restricted to "no more than 3 glasses between 6 & 10pm". After lying empty for a period, the premises were converted to a licensed club in the 1970s, and subsequently to a pub. Formerly the 'Model Tavern', since the 1990s it has been known as the Sportsman.

West View Hotel — *Mansfield Road*

Formerly a Tennants Brewery house at Hillstown, ownership had passed to the Laurel Pub Company before it was closed in 2004.

White Swan

Market Place

The original White Swan c.1920.

This historic pub is at least 600 years old, as evidenced by an original beam in the back room, making it one of the oldest pubs in North East Derbyshire. Until the early 1900s the inn had recognisable Tudor windows and a stone roof, with a massive chimney rising right up one side of the building. The true age of the pub came to light when an architect made a thorough investigation and discovered an oak-framed structure on the old 'cruck' principal, underneath the stone exterior. Indeed it was found that there were wooden posts from ground to roof level, with cross beams for carrying the first floor, and that the stone facing was merely a shell. Because the building depended for its strength on this wooden structure, it was decided that alterations were impractical and the decision was taken to rebuild the pub completely. When this eventually took place in the late 1920s, a carved oak beam from the front bar was re-positioned in the roof of one of the rear rooms. The carvings are said to date the beam as late 15th century.

The pub's owners, Hardy's Kimberley Brewery, which subsequently was Hardys & Hansons until the brewery was unnecessarily closed by Greene King in December 2006, produced a booklet to commemorate the significant alterations that were made to the pub and this has been used in this article. Greene King beers may now be enjoyed in these historic surroundings.

BONSALL

One of the earliest mentions of a settlement at 'Bonteshale' was in 1297. By the 16th century the village was known as 'Bonsall' or 'Bonsale', and it prospered as a result of lead mining. Licensing records at the County Record Office (Matlock) for 1776 show 12 victuallers and the first Trade Directory in 1821/2 lists 6 inns. Times have moved on and although only two pubs now remain open, at least four of the ex-pubs are still standing.

Barley Mow pictured here in 1983. [John Hirst]

Barley Mow

[John Hirst]

The Dale
The Barley Mow premises were converted into a pub around 1819, when Thomas Millward bought a miner's cottage for £140. The pub was famous for once having a 'Rock Cellar' at ground level, literally hewn out of the rock. Robert Hanson of Kimberley, one half of the business that later became Hardys & Hansons Brewery, bought the pub in 1898 for £1250, a significant amount in those days. Moving forward to the 20th Century, the Barley Mow was the first ever Chesterfield CAMRA branch Pub of the Year in 1983, while run by Dennis and Barbara Bark (pictured left), and owned by Hardys & Hansons. Having been closed during the period 1986-89, the pub was subsequently renovated and the old bar above floor level was removed. The pub retains its original charm, serves excellent real ale and food, and is the home of the 'World Hen Racing Championships' which are held every August in the pub car park.

Britannia
The Britannia can be traced back to the 18th century and it is also known that the last recorded landlord, William Spencer, was also a butcher. The pub closed in the early 1870s.

King's Head

Helen Frances

Yeoman Street
Generally accepted as being the oldest inn in Bonsall and said to date back to 1649, when King Charles lost his head, the current premises in front of the historic market cross were built in 1677. The first landlord, John Abell, engraved his name on a wooden beam above the entrance when his first son was born. Many subsequent generations of Abells were also landlords at the pub. It has been owned by a number of breweries - Strettons (taken over 1927), Ind Coope, Allsop and Ansells (in the 1980s). The pub is now one of only a handful of pubs in Derbyshire belonging to Bateman's Brewery of Wainfleet, having been acquired by them in 1999. A range of Bateman's beers may now be enjoyed in this atmospheric pub.

Miners' Standard

High Street
The Miners' Standard, which was situated at 17-19 High Street, closed sometime during the period 1904-1908, although the premises are still standing. The name reflects the historical importance of lead mining to Bonsall. A noticeable trend from looking at Trade Directory records is that the same landlord is rarely listed twice and possibly the Miners Standard always struggled to provide its landlords with sufficient income.

Pig of Lead   *Clatterway*

If you enter Bonsall from the A5012 (also known as the Via Gellia) and take the road known as 'Clatterway', immediately on the left hand side is an imposing three story building which used to be the Pig of Lead until it closed in 1995. Indeed, the name is still engraved on the lintel above the door. The pub was also known as the Via Gellia Inn during the period 1876-1912 and was once owned by Home Brewery. The pub's name was inspired by the local lead mining industry, 'pig' being a term for an oblong mass of unpurified metal, obtained in the smelting process.

New Inn/Fountain Inn   *Yeoman Street*

The former Fountain Inn. [Neil Parkin]

The New Inn was first recorded as being open in 1846 and was situated at 1 Yeoman Street, at the junction of Clatterway/Yeoman Street and the road to Bonsall Dale. The first landlord, Josiah Oliver, remained at the pub for the whole of the period 1846-1881 and had a number of other business interests, as he was also a grocer, fruiterer and carrier. The name change to Fountain Inn occurred around 1884, and was inspired by its position near the Victorian-Gothic drinking fountain. Although the pub closed in the 1980s the post that held its signboard is still visible. The last known landlord, Mr. Shaposka Sharman, was Polish and an ex-fighter pilot.

Queen's Head   *Yeoman Street*

Next door to the Kings Head at 64 The Cross/Yeoman Street is a private residence that now houses a violin business. Formerly the Queen's Head, and owned by Derby brewers Alton & Co., it closed in 1817 under the Compensation Act. The premises were initially converted into a fish and chip shop.

Lillies Inn   *Ible*

First recorded as the Lillies Inn in 1870 when the landlord was named as one John Hardy. He was also a corn miller. The pub was situated further up the Via Gellia from Bonsall at Ible near Grangemill. Little is known about the pub apart from the fact that the licence was not renewed in 1956 because it was considered uneconomic to carry out improvements. However, there was a licensed victualler (Samuel Hinder or Kinder) recorded at Ible in 1809 indicating that the pub may date back to the 18th, or early 19th century.

Gate   *Slaley*

Little is known about this pub other than it was mentioned in Trade Directories for 1864 & 1876 and that it was located in the small hamlet of Slaley.

BRIMINGTON

Situated two miles to the north east of Chesterfield, the development of Brimington's inns and pubs has been influenced by its transport links. Early travellers used the stagecoaches to and from Gainsborough and Manchester that passed through the village whilst the Chesterfield Canal, built in the late 1770s, passes nearby. Two further events occurred in 1841 when Brimington Common was enclosed and the road to Calow surveyed. Many of the pubs built to serve these travellers have survived into the 21st century.

Ark Tavern   *Chesterfield Road*

Built in 1808, as confirmed by a date engraved in a stone in one of the gable ends, the Ark

Tavern was originally a Wesleyan Methodist Chapel. Whilst it is not known when the premises were converted to a beerhouse, the building's previous use could be the source of the 'Ark Tavern' name with its religious link. Previous owners have included Tennant Brothers' Brewery of Sheffield and the Ark is one of a limited number of pubs in the area that is still owned by a brewery, in this case Thwaites of Blackburn.

Brickmakers' Arms   *Manor Road*
This ex-Stones pub opened as a beerhouse in the 1860s and remains open today.

Bugle Horn   *Hall Road*

*Taken c.1910. The landlord, Mr. Watson, is in the front row next to the boy (his son). The tall man in the middle of the back row (with flat cap) is John William Keeling, subsequently killed in action on 25th August 1916 during the First World War.
(Mr. A. P. Harrison and Local Studies Section, Chesterfield Library).*

A coaching inn that dates back to the 18th century, it was one of only two pubs in Brimington in 1828. At that time it was run by John & Mary Greaves who had been licensees since the early 1800s. The pub was situated on Hall Road and closed in 1927 whilst owned by Chesterfield Brewery and the licence transferred to the Hollingwood Hotel. After closure the premises were converted to a private dwelling house before being demolished. Brimington Clinic now occupies the site.

Butchers' Arms   *Church Street*
First listed in 1852. The name is derived from the fact that the first known licensee, William Siddall, was also a butcher. The pub, which is still open, was originally a Richdales' house but via takeovers ownership passed in turn to Hammonds, Northern United Breweries and Bass Charrington.

Canal Tavern   Frog Row

Canal Tavern prior to demolition. [John Hirst collection]

The Canal Tavern was a beerhouse that used to be situated next to the Chesterfield Canal (north bank), at the side of Staveley Works. When it closed in 1963, the Derbyshire Times faithfully recorded the event. It was reported that this: "half-forgotten" pub was due to close on 4th April and was then to be demolished. The landlord at that time was a Mr. Alfred Ernest Crane. The pub, which sold Gilmours Brewery beers, also had stabling for four horses and these were no doubt used when boatmen rested at the Tavern for the night. In terms of location, Staveley Works was said to be 'in the pub's backyard' and the pub came right up to the edge of the canal.

Corner House   High Street
The Corner House is the new boy on the block, having opened in July 1998 after being converted from a shop.

Markham Arms   Dorset Drive
This is another ex-Stones's pub, which opened in 1957, and is hidden away on Dorset Drive, New Brimington.

Mill   Station Road
Previously known as the New Inn (until 1903/4) and the Great Central (until 1991), the Mill is situated in pleasant surroundings next to the Chesterfield Canal. In March 1886 a gruesome murder occurred near the pub. The victim was Mr. Herbert Crookes, a businessman who lived near Cutthorpe. On the night in question, Mr. Crookes was heading home along the canal towpath from Clowne. A boy at "the nearby New Inn" heard screams about 11.30pm. Whilst it is known that robbery was the motive for the attack, the murderers were never caught. As at 2007, the landlord was Peter Swan, the ex-Sheffield Wednesday and England footballer and the pub's signboard shows Peter in his England strip.

Miners' Arms   *Manor Road*

The Miners' Arms was first mentioned in Trade Directories in 1857 as a beerhouse run by William Salmon and situated at Brimington Common. By 1864, it held a full licence, with Salmon still as licensee. The pub's 20th century history includes being owned by the Chesterfield Brewery until it was taken over by Mansfield Brewery in 1935 which, in turn, sold it to Burtonwood Brewery in 1989. Following a further takeover, the pub is now owned by Marston's (previously known as Wolverhampton & Dudley Breweries).

Prince of Wales   *Manor Road*

Helen Frances
The Prince of Wales as it looked in 2001.

The Prince of Wales opened in the 1860s as a beerhouse and originally sold Scarsdale Brewery beers. The pub has changed name three times. The first change came in the late 1960s/early 1970s when it became known as the Brimington Tavern. Then in the late 1970s, a further change was made and the pub became known as 'The Warren', until another owner finally saw some sense and reverted back to its original name in 1984. The pub was an outlet for Oakwell Brewery beers from Barnsley until it closed in 2007 after planning consent was given for houses to be built on the site.

Red Lion   *Church Street*

Formerly owned by Chesterfield Brewery, the Red Lion is the second oldest surviving pub in Brimington, having first been listed in 1835.

Three Horseshoes   *High Street*

Records confirm that the Three Horseshoes is the oldest surviving pub in Brimington as it can be traced back to the 18th century from licensing applications. Brewery ties have included Chesterfield and Mansfield Breweries. It was originally a coaching inn, a fact confirmed by the 'Three Horseshoes' name that has long been associated with coaching inns. In his book, 'British Inn Signs' (1972), author Eric Delderfield offers the following explanation:

"Inns bearing the sign of THREE HORSESHOES are numerous and more often than not they are to be found after a long stretch of road without habitation. Probably the inn grew up as a neighbour to a blacksmith, who could always find business in replacing a missing shoe".

Victoria Hotel   *King Street*

The Victoria Hotel was situated on King Street. Renewal of its licence was refused in 1869 when the licensee was George Steel.

COAL ASTON

Bulmer's Trade Directory for 1895 describes Coal Aston as: "situated on an eminence 1 mile N.E of Dronfield and is chiefly occupied by colliers". A coal mine in Coal Aston had opened in 1785. There are various theories about the name – that it is a corruption of 'Cold Aston', and refers to the village's exposed position, although local historian Kathryn Battye suggests that the name means 'old eastern farm'. Records indicate that Coal Aston has never had more than four public houses and, unusually, they are all still open.

Chequers   Eckington Road

The oldest pub in the village as evidenced by an 1821/2 Trade Directory which listed 'William Tomlinson vict. Chequers', the only such entry for Coal Aston. The pub was acquired in 1855 by the Sheffield brewery Thomas Rawson & Co. who owned it, and the Royal Oak down the road until the brewery and its pub estate was acquired by Gilmours Brewery in the mid-20th century. A well-known landlord, Charlie Jessop, was at the pub for the period 1952-77. At that time the pub was a basic village local and it is only in more recent years that it developed into a family eatery with attached children's play barn. Whilst change is inevitable, it may not always be for the best!

Cross Daggers   Brown Lane

Cross Daggers c.1910.
[Bob Gratton collection]

Owned by Whitmarsh, Watson & Co of Sheffield, subsequently acquired by Gilmours, until the early 20th century. It is still open, hidden away on Brown Lane.

Royal Oak   Eckington Road

Known locally as the 'Pond', in view of the duck pond which stood across the road from the pub, and a beerhouse until the 1940s, the Royal Oak served Rawson's ales and stout until that brewery was taken over by Gilmours in the 1950s. The landlord in the 1950s and 60s, Wally Harrop, also worked on the local club circuit as a stand up comedian and performed his act at the pub, to full houses, apparently. The pub, minus pond, is still open as at 2007 and you can try the traditional pub pastime of 'Ringing the Bull' – a game that involves swinging a metal ring attached to the roof on a piece of string towards a hook attached to the wall.

Yew Tree — Holmely Lane

Yew Tree at the beginning of the 20th century.
[Bob Gratton collection]

A William Stones's beerhouse that dates back to the 19th century, and is now owned by Enterprise Inns.

CROMFORD

The original settlement of 'Crunforde', meaning crooked ford, was by the River Derwent in an area now known as Cromford Bridge, where the local church still stands. Most people will be aware of Richard Arkwright's association with Cromford, it is not exactly easy to pass through and miss both of his two former mills...!; but perhaps not everyone will be aware that the novelist Alison Uttley lived there as a child. Whilst Ms. Uttley did not influence the opening of any pubs, Richard Arkwright and his successors certainly did by building many of them.

In the area we now think of as Cromford, there was an ancient lead mining settlement known as Scarthin, dominated by a rock formation that blocked direct access to Matlock Bath. In 1790 a narrow passageway was blasted through the rock, followed by further clearance in the 1820s, which enabled a road, later the A6, to be built. Scarthin Rocks are the remnants of what was once a considerable barrier.

Cromford today is an attractive, interesting and lively town. It is well worth the effort of a visit, especially if you look beyond the main street and discover remnants of the Cromford that existed before Mr. Arkwright arrived.

Bell Inn — Cromford Hill

The Bell was one of two pubs that stood on either side of North Street at its junction with Cromford Hill, the Cock Inn being the other. Richard Arkwright built the street in 1776-7 to house mill workers, but it is not clear if the pubs opened around this time. It is said that Arkwright encouraged his workers (and their children) to drink beer rather than the local water supply as the latter suffered from lead contamination. The earliest known landlord (1828), James Gell, was also a maltster and it is possible that he brewed beer on the premises. At that time, the pub was known as the Blue Bell, the more simplified 'Bell' name being used since the late 1840s. The pub was part of the Hardys & Hansons estate that was bought by Greene King in 2006 and is a fine example of a traditional Derbyshire local, with two cask-conditioned beers available.

Boat Inn *Scarthin*

Boat Inn. [Glynn Waite collection]

Situated on Scarthin (now a street name) near to the mill pond, the Boat Inn was built about 1772 as a flour merchant business, although some parts of the building are said to be older. By the early 1830s it was being used as a beerhouse, known as the New Inn. The first known landlord, Anthony Boden, was also a butcher. Later the name changed to the Hit or Miss, which could possibly be a reference to inconsistent beer quality. At an auction in September 1865 the pub was described as a: "freehold beer-house and dwelling-house at Scarthen Row recently called 'Hit or Miss' and now called 'The Boat', comprising ... brewhouse, slaughterhouse ...". It belonged to William Allen, who had changed the name of the beerhouse since he was a boatman on the Cromford Canal. The pub was granted a full licence in 1954 and belonged to, or was leased, by Offilers Brewery (Derby) during the 20th century. During the 1990s it operated as a freehouse until it was sold in 2006 to Punch Taverns. A selection of real ales is available.

Bull's Head *Scarthin*

Scarthin was well populated in the 18th and 19th centuries and was able to support the Bull's Head and two beerhouses, see the Boat and Wheatsheaf. The Bull's Head was the oldest of these, as confirmed by Trade Directory records and also by the fact that it held a full licence, as beerhouse licences were only available from 1830 onwards. The pub, now demolished, stood at the bottom (Market Place) end of Scarthin. Some writers have suggested that the Bull's Head was an earlier name for the Boat Inn, but a review of the documentary evidence available shows that both pubs were in existence at the same time. Whilst the exact date of closure is unknown, the pub ceased being mentioned in records in the 1880s.

Cock Inn *Cromford Hill*

Former Cock Inn c.1910 pictured when a tea room. [Glynn Waite collection]

Situated on North Street at the opposite corner to the Bell and now a private residence, 43&45 Cromford Hill, the Cock Inn was one of five Cromford pubs included in an 1828 Trade Directory. The earliest known landlord, John Mart, was also listed as a carrier (1828) and a farmer (1860). An 1888 Rate book shows a Mrs Marie ---- as the proprietor, the surnames on part of this page have been cut out. She was Mrs Marie Statham who is shown as a refreshment-room keeper in an 1895 Trade Directory. From the information available, it appears that Mrs Statham surrendered the licence in 1893 and the premises were then used as a tea room. This is supported by a postcard, dated about 1910, which shows a refreshment room sign outside the building.

Crown Inn   *Cromford Hill*

The Crown was recorded as a public house in trade directories for the period 1828-1842, but the exact date and reason for closing are not known. The only known landlord, Joshua Roper, was also a wheelwright. Situated towards the bottom of Cromford Hill, between 'Cromford Newsagents' and 'Janets', the premises were subsequently used by a butcher and then as a shop called 'Collectors' Corner'. The building is now a private residence.

George and Dragon   *Cromford Bridge*

A beerhouse, the George & Dragon was only listed in 1835 & 1842.

Greyhound Hotel   *Market Place*

Originally called the Black Greyhound and built as a hotel in 1778 by Richard Arkwright to house businessmen and other visitors to Cromford, the Greyhound provided a focal point for village activities, although it is said that mill workers were not allowed inside. The pub has also been known locally as the 'Black Dog' and in an 1828 Trade Directory, it was described as a commercial inn and coach house.

Greyhound Hotel c.1910. [Glynn Waite collection]

Edmund Bradbury (1880), describing a journey on the Cromford & High Peak Railway, wrote that: "The Greyhound at Cromford is eloquent of a refreshing bath, and of a well-cooked dish of plump trout that were rising at flies in the cool Derwent an hour ago." Matthew Hill, of the Cromford Brewery, was the proprietor for some years before the brewery re-located to Cromford Mill. The hotel still stands in the Market Place and recently has been owned by Hardys & Hansons (2003-6) and subsequently, Greene King.

Junction Inn   *High Peak Junction*

The Junction Inn was a public house, in the vicinity of Lea Mills, which existed for about 40 years. Before becoming a pub, it may have been a property known as 'Hobson's House', which is shown on early maps at the same spot later occupied by the pub. Owned by the Arkwright family, it was first listed in an 1846 Trade Directory as a pub/inn, the first known landlord being Samuel Brown. The final listing for the pub that has been discovered was in 1881, when the landlord was James Brown. This gentleman was still listed in 1888, although his occupation is given as 'farmer'. Indeed, the licence may have stayed in the same family as a Francis Smedley Brown is recorded as the landlord for the period 1852-62. The 'Junction' name originates from the pub's location at High Peak Junction, approximately one mile south east of Cromford Village

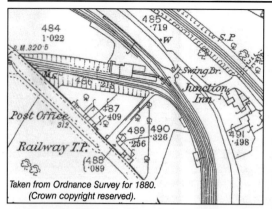

Taken from Ordnance Survey for 1880.
(Crown copyright reserved).

on the A6. It was here that the Cromford & High Peak Railway (completed in 1831) had its original terminus and it was also the point where it met up with the Cromford Canal, enabling goods to be transported from canal to railway and vice versa. The pub was situated on a thin strip of land between the canal and the Midland Railway. In the 1880s the Midland Railway Company decided to straighten the track in the High Peak Junction area and, to achieve this, the pub was demolished. The nearby railway cutting and bridge both bear the name 'Brown' in honour of the last landlord, James Brown.

King's Head   *Masson Mill*
Richard Arkwright also built Masson Mill, just up the road from Cromford, although it actually falls in Matlock parish. The King's Head, described as a three-storey Georgian Inn, stood at the side of Masson Mill. The inn was listed in the earliest trade directory for the area (1828) and was last recorded as open in 1857. By 1862 it was stated as being empty and subsequently became a private house, until it was demolished in the 1970s to allow the main road (A6) to be widened.

Miner's Standard   *Bolehill (Wirksworth)*
The Miner's Standard was the oldest of four pubs that used to be found in Bolehill, situated midway between Cromford and Wirksworth. This was once an important lead mining area (a Bole is a furnace for smelting lead) and a number of mines were found nearby. The pub's name is a reference to the standard dish, used to measure the lead that a miner had extracted in order to calculate its value. An outlet for Offilers Brewery beers of Derby, the pub closed in the 1990s and was converted into a private house.

Railway Inn   *Steeple Houses (Wirksworth)*
The Railway Inn was situated in the area known as Steeple Houses at the top of Cromford Hill. At this point, the bridge that carried the Cromford & High Peak Railway (C&HPR) across the Wirksworth road can still be found. The building next to it at the junction of Steeple Grange and Oakerthorpe Road was once the Railway Inn, just inside Wirksworth parish. Originally known as the Cromford & High Peak Railway Inn and thought to have been built by the Arkwright family, the pub was recorded as being open as early as 1828, before the C&HPR was operational. For many years in the 19th century it was in the hands of the Howsley (also spelt Houseley) family, who were also farmers. Whilst the exact date and reason for closure are not known, the pub was no longer open by the early 1920s.

Red Lion   *Cromford Hill*
The Red Lion was a public house that was only open for around 30 years in the middle of the 19th century. The only known landlord, George Eaton, was also a farmer. The building, now a private house, is situated half way up Cromford Hill on the left-hand side just below the junction with Barnwell Lane.

Un-named pub/beerhouse   *Cromford Hill*
It is thought that there may have been a pub or beerhouse on Cromford Hill at its junction with Bakers Lane. No further details are known.

Rutland Arms

Masson Mill

Taken c.1910, the Rutland Arms is at the far end of the row. [Ken Smith collection]

The Rutland Arms, a mill workers pub first recorded in 1842, stood in a terraced row directly opposite Masson Mill. A substantial 3-storey building, it was demolished, along with adjacent 2-storey houses that also made up the terrace, to allow the main road (A6) to be widened in the 1970s. The last known landlord, Ossie Whittaker, also supplied bottled ale for the weekly dances in the Pavilion at Matlock Bath. The pub had a pinball machine in the 1960s and there was a small prize, e.g. a packet of cigarettes, for the highest score of the day.

Thorn Tree   Steeple Houses (Wirksworth)

A beerhouse situated at Steeple Houses, the Thorn Tree was only listed in 1842.

Wheatsheaf   Scarthin

According to the history board in the Boat Inn, a beerhouse known as the 'Wheatsheaf' was situated at Scarthin Nick, along with the Bull's Head, and in 1841 was kept by Matthew Beastall. It is not known when it closed.

So who was Arkwright…?

Sir Richard Arkwright (1732-1792) is generally given the credit for being the founder of the modern factory system. However, before be built the first of his two cotton mills at Cromford in 1771, he had held down roles as diverse as a peruke (wig) maker and landlord, apparently an unsuccessful one, losing money on alterations to the public house in question. Not exactly the sort of CV you might expect from a man who became a prominent 18th century industrialist. He is credited with a number of inventions that enabled the cotton industry to be mechanised, most notably the 'water frame' cotton spinning machine. However, his critics assert that he was never slow to take other's ideas and then claim them as his own. Arkwright died a very rich man, thanks not only to his inventions, but also to the industry of the Derbyshire people who worked in his mills. He left an estate valued at around half a million pounds, not a bad return on the £500 that he borrowed in the early 1770s to build Cromford mill.

…and what was the Cromford & High Peak Railway (C&HPR)?

An 1825 Act of Parliament authorised the construction of a railway, or tram road, to link the Cromford Canal with the Peak Forest Canal at Whaley Bridge. And so, despite the steep climbs that would have to be negotiated, the C&HPR was born. This first section was opened in 1830, although the C&HPR was not a 'railway' in the conventional sense, as engines could not climb the steep inclines required to enable the track to reach 950 feet at its highest point at Ladmanlow. Instead, stationary winding engines were used to pull trucks up these steeper sections. On flatter sections, horses and later steam engines were used. Indeed, it could take up to 16 hours to complete the end to end journey of 33 miles! In 1853 the railway was extended to meet the Midland Railway to become part of the national railway system. However, by the 1960s, goods traffic had become almost non-existent and the line was closed in April 1967. The route survives as the 'High Peak Trail' and the winding house at Middleton Top still has a working engine.

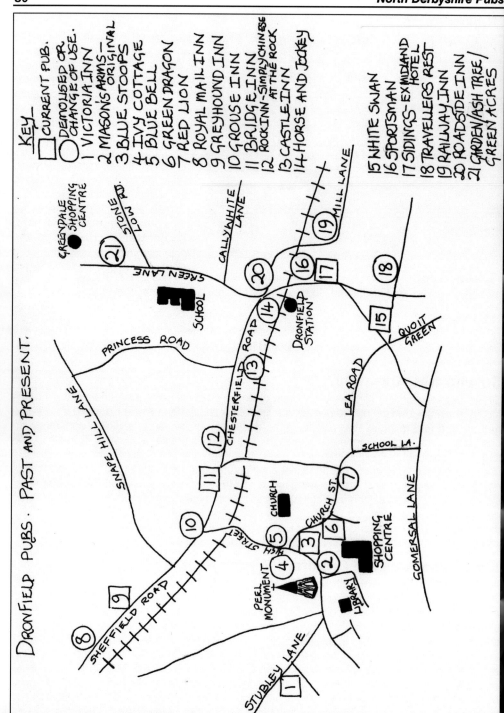

Past and Present 31

DRONFIELD

Situated between Sheffield and Chesterfield, Dronfield was already in existence at the time of the 1086 Domesday Book and its name is thought to mean, 'the open land where there are male bees (drones)'. The majority of pubs in the town developed around the main Sheffield/Chesterfield Road. However, the oldest pubs may be found in the vicinity of the church and Peel Monument, which is situated on High Street and was built in 1854 to commemorate the repeal of the Corn Laws in 1846 by Sir Robert Peel. Nearby is the modern shopping precinct and Civic Centre.

Blue Bell   Church Street

This John Smiths' beerhouse closed in December 1912 when its licence expired and was not renewed. The substantial premises were situated at the bottom of High Street - on an early 20th century pub crawl it would have come between the Blue Stoops and the Green Dragon. The Blue Bell was demolished in the late 1920s/early 1930s.

Blue Bell c.1910.
[Bob Gratton collection]

Blue Stoops   High Street

The Blue Stoops is one of the oldest pubs in Dronfield – as confirmed by a date-stone of 1596 over the fire place – although the pub was rebuilt in the 18th century. It is also referred to as the 'Blue Posts' in Trade Directories, a reference to the old practice of painting door pillars/posts to identify a property. The pub was owned by Wards Brewery for many years.

Bowshaw   Sheffield Road

The large family-orientated food pub that is now the Bowshaw, situated at the top of the Dronfield by-pass, was known as the Nag's Head until the mid 1990s. Further back in time, it was owned by Bentley's Old Brewery of Rotherham until the middle of the 20th century. Records often refer to it as being situated at 'Birchett', an old name for the area and, historically, part of Unstone. It is now a 'Toby Carvery' restaurant/pub.

Bridge Inn   Sheffield Road

Opened sometime during the period 1840-1870 and initially, may have held a beerhouse licence only. By the early 20th century a full licence had been granted and it was owned by Carter, Milner & Bird, better known as Hope Brewery (later to become Hope & Anchor Brewery) - famous for its Jubilee Stout. The pub is still open.

Bridge Inn prior to the railway opening in 1870.
[Bob Gratton collection]

Castle Inn   *Chesterfield Road*

Castle Inn seen c.1920. [Bob Gratton collection]

This beerhouse was situated on the main road, roughly opposite to where Princess Road joins. It closed in the 1920s, when owned by Sheffield Brewer, Thomas Berry & Co., and the frontage of the building reduced to allow the road to be widened. The rear portion of the building has survived and a new, smaller, frontage added.

Coach & Horses   *Sheffield Road*

Coach & Horses taken c.1905. The Toll Bar Cottage seen on the left has since been demolished. [Bob Gratton collection]

Built circa 1797 when an alternative turnpike route to Sheffield, that passed along the Drone Valley towards Bowshaw and onto Sheffield, was constructed. This replaced the original route that left Dronfield via Green lane in the direction of Coal Aston. Accordingly it was originally a coaching inn, and there were stables next to the pub, where car park is now. The first known landlord was Samuel Priestley (early 1820s). The pub has had a multitude of owners, mainly, but not exclusively, breweries. They include Wards, Tomlinsons and Scarsdale (1950s) In 2006 it was bought by the world's oldest football club, Sheffield FC, who play on the ground behind the pub. A half-time pint of beer from the independent Thornbridge Brewery from Derbyshire, which now supplies the pub, is an added attraction.

Cricketers   *Hill Top*

Also known as the Cricketers' Arms, this beerhouse closed in October 1914 when its licence expired and was not renewed. It could be found near the top of Gomersal Lane and was owned by Tomlinson's Anchor Brewery at the time of closure. As an aside, the German Luftwaffe destroyed the Anchor Brewery in 1940, which lead to a merger with Carter, Milne & Bird and the creation of the Hope & Anchor Brewery.

Garden   *Green Lane*

The 'Garden' was previously called the 'Ash Tree' (until 2005) and prior to that, 'Green Acres'. This was a relatively new pub, as it opened in 1969. To avoid increasing the number of pubs in the area, the licence for the new pub was transferred from the Red Lion on Church Street. As at 2007, the pub was closed and was in the process of being converted to a restaurant.

Green Dragon   *Church Street*

Helen Frances

An ancient treasure that can be found in North Derbyshire! The Green Dragon is one of Dronfield's most historic buildings and most likely, its oldest surviving inn. It was formerly a medieval Chantry House used by priests from Beauchief Abbey that probably included a brew house at the rear. It is thought that it became an alehouse in the 16th or early 17th century, when it was also rebuilt and extended. A visit is recommended to fully appreciate its age, as evidenced by the huge stone fireplace. Unfortunately you can no longer access the underground passageway that links the pub's cellar and a family vault that is situated inside the church across the road as this was sealed during the 20th Century. The pub is sometimes referred to in records as the 'Dragon' and John Smith's and Stones's Breweries have been previous owners.

Greyhound Inn   *Sheffield Road*

Following the opening of the second turnpike road in 1797, the subsequent growth in the number of travellers passing through Dronfield lead to the opening of two new inns – the Greyhound and the Royal Mail (see below). The Greyhound was also known as the 'Halfway House' as it was equidistant between Sheffield and Chesterfield. The Greyhound was one of eight Dronfield inns listed in Pigot's 1821/2 Trade Directory and for many years it was owned by Tennants' Brewery of Sheffield. As at March 2008 the pub was closed, with a sign outside stating that it would be re-opening as a Thai restaurant.

Grouse Inn   *Sheffield Road*

A Brampton Brewery beerhouse, the Grouse closed in December 1920 when its licence expired. The premises, situated on Sheffield Road close to the Snape Hill Lane junction, were demolished in the 1930s.

Horse & Jockey   *Chesterfield Road*

This coaching inn was situated opposite the junction of Green Lane and Chesterfield Road, and was built to serve travellers on the original turnpike route, which reached Dronfield by following the route of the present-day Green Lane. It was situated near a tollbar and would have supplied fresh horses to the stagecoaches from its own stables. It is also said that two elephants were once stabled in a shed in the back yard during a visit by the circus in the 1920s! A Tennant's Brewery pub, it was closed and demolished in the 1930s.

Hyde Park Inn   Hilltop Road
There is not a great deal of information available on the Hyde Park Inn which is still open and is part of the Enterprise Inns Pub Company. The pub is situated on the hill above Dronfield and owners have included Tomlinsons and Hope & Anchor Breweries, both of Sheffield.

Ivy Cottage   High Street
A beerhouse owned by John Smiths brewery and which closed in 1912, the Ivy Cottage was situated on High Street on what is now a vacant plot, next to Samad's Indian Restaurant. This 17th century property, which was indeed covered in ivy, was demolished in the 1930s.

Mason's Arms   Farwater Lane

The original Mason's Arms in the 1920s. [Bob Gratton collection]

The original Mason's Arms has been described by author Roger Redfern ('Britain in Old Photographs – Dronfield') as: "A beautifully proportioned, gabled Elizabethan house beside Farwater Lane, pulled down soon after the Second World War." A beerhouse owned by Stones Brewery, it stood near to the entrance to the current Civic Centre car park. The old pub, said to be the only one in Dronfield with its own skittle alley, closed in the 1930s and the licence was transferred to a new pub of the same name at the junction of Chesterfield & Cemetery Road.

Mason's Arms/Hallowes   Cemetery Road
When the original Mason's Arms closed in the 1930s, the licence was transferred to this re-incarnation. It was one of three pubs, built in mock-Tudor fashion at this time by Stones Brewery, the others being the Hearts of Oak (Dronfield Woodhouse) and the Blackamoor (Troway). In 2003 it was renamed as the Hallowes.

One Bar   Lea Road
A modern, trendy wine bar that opened circa c.2005. Say no more.

Railway   Mill Lane
A beerhouse belonging to William Stones's Brewery that was also known as the 'Tap'. One of three pubs on Mill Lane, it was reputed to serve the best Stones ale for miles around, attributed to its deep and cold beer cellar. It closed in 1958 when its licence was surrendered.

Red Lion   Church Street
The Red Lion was situated at the junction of Church Street and Lea Road, close to and on the same side of the road as the Green Dragon. It dated back to the beginning of the 18th century, possibly earlier, was well-known for having a snooker

Railway Inn late 1920s. [Bob Gratton collection]

hall on the first floor, and in 1898 it was acquired by Old Albion Brewery. The pub closed in 1969 and its licence was transferred to the Green Acres, also in Dronfield. Whilst the pub had often suffered from flooding, the eventual reason for closure was due to concerns about the road junction being dangerous. Accordingly, the building was demolished for road widening and an area of grass left where the pub once stood.

Red Lion and "The Knott" in the 1920s.
[Bob Gratton collection]

Roadside Inn — Mill Lane
A free house, the Roadside Inn stood at the end of Mill Lane. The site is now occupied by a Nat West Bank. A surviving photograph shows the pub walls advertising 'James Haynes & Co Crown Ales & Beers'. This Sheffield brewery ceased trading in 1915.

Rock Inn — Chesterfield Road
Another Stones beerhouse in Dronfield that opened sometime after 1830. It remained as a beerhouse until 1950 when a full licence was granted. It is said that it was a "rough and basic type of establishment" into the 1960s. It is now a Chinese restaurant.

Royal Mail Inn — Sheffield Road
This coaching inn was situated along from the Greyhound, near to the junction of Sheffield Road and Holmley Lane, and was another stopping point for stagecoaches (and also Royal Mail coaches, if the name is anything to go by). It was built later than the Greyhound, and its useful life seems to have been curtailed as the railways took the trade of the stagecoaches. Photographic evidence confirms that the inn was still trading around the 1860s, but it does not appear in Pub Licence records for the early 20th century and so the conclusion is that it closed before the end of the 19th century.

Sidings — Chesterfield Road
Previously known as the Midland Hotel until the 1980s, the Sidings has been owned by Truswell's Brewery, Sheffield and passed, via a company takeover, to Hope & Anchor Brewery and ultimately to Bass. It is now a freehouse. It has also been known as the 'Old Sidings', but the 'Old' prefix appears to have been dropped. In doing this, the owners have bucked a trend, as many other licensees seem to want to introduce 'Old/Olde into their pub's name. Why?

Sportsman — Mill Lane
The final stop for alcoholic refreshment on Mill Lane was the Sportsman, which stood opposite the Roadside Inn. A beerhouse, it closed when its licence expired in October 1914. At the beginning of the 20th century it was owned by Whitmarsh, Watson & Co., Sheffield, which was acquired by Duncan Gilmour & Co. in 1906.

Traveller's Rest — Chesterfield Road
A beerhouse that once could be found on Chesterfield Road, across from where the White Swan still stands. It was owned by Greaves Brewery, Sheffield and closed in the early part of the 20th century, but the building has survived.

Victoria Inn — Stubley Lane
Originally a 19th century beerhouse, owners of the Victoria have included John Smiths (up to 1904) and Duncan Gilmour & Co., who acquired it in 1914. Latterly it has been owned by Banks's, now part of the Marston's Group, and their beers can now be enjoyed in the pub.

White Swan — *Chesterfield Road*
Its listing in an 1827/9 Trade Directory makes the White Swan one of the older Dronfield pubs, so it is surprising that it is rarely mentioned in accounts of 19th and 20th century life in the town. It has been owned by Thomas Berry & Co and Tennant's Brewery (both of Sheffield), amongst others.

DRONFIELD WOODHOUSE
Although most people know Dronfield Woodhouse as a large housing development - it was the largest privately owned housing estate in Europe when it was built in the 1970s - a 13th century house is evidence that the area was been inhabited much earlier, while coal mining arrived in the area in 1795. The first two beerhouses in the area were recorded in 1833.

Hearts of Oak — *Northern Common*
A beerhouse that was completely rebuilt in the 1930s, resulting in the mock-Tudor fronted pub in existence today. This was one of three William Stones's pubs that were rebuilt at the same time, to a very similar design. The others were the Blackamoor (Troway) and the Mason's Arms (Dronfield). See those entries for further information.

Jolly Farmer — *Pentland Road*
Opened as 'The Gorsey Brigg' in November 1976, originally selling beers from the now defunct Nottingham brewer, Shipstones. The pub was refurbished in 1998, the name changed to 'Jolly Farmer' and now has a reputation locally for serving some of the best quality beer in the area.

Miner's Arms — *Carr Lane*
Still open today; the Miner's was an Old Albion house until that brewery was acquired by Duncan Gilmour & Co. in 1919.

Talbot Arms — *Stubley Lane*
The original Talbot Arms was a John Smiths' beerhouse (a full licence being granted in 1946). Permission was then granted in 1967 for the pub to be rebuilt, which has resulted in the current modern pub.

ECKINGTON
At the risk of appearing sentimental, let's wind back the clock and remember some of the 'lost' pubs of Eckington.

Apollo/Royal Hotel — *Southgate*
From a review of Trade Directories, and using a process of deduction, it can be stated with some certainty that the Apollo existed between 1833 and 1876. The licensee in 1876 was Leonard Lund. By 1879 Lund was running the Royal Hotel, also in Eckington; there is no evidence that both pubs were open at the same time. There are at least two possibilities here; the pub may have been renamed, or alternatively the Apollo closed and Lund moved to a new pub. The Royal Hotel still stands but closed in 2006.

Royal Hotel 1904. Note from the sign that it was also a Parcels Office for the Mdland Railway. [Dave Matthews collection]

Brown Bear   *Market Street*

Situated at 26 Market Street, this pub closed in 1915 when leased to Gilmours Brewery. It was also known as the 'Bear', as shown in Trade Directories for 1821-7 and 1835, while the 16th February 1861 edition of the Derbyshire Times reported that an inquest opened at the 'Bear Inn' on the body of John Brown, a miner, aged 22. The 1795 Fairbank Survey of Eckington shows a pub called the 'White Bear' – possibly this was the same pub.

Coach & Horses   *Rotherham Road*

Originally a 15th or 16th century alehouse, it is thought to have been the "poor sorry inn" at "Ackington" that the writer and traveller Celia Fiennes stopped at in 1697 – her travel memoirs were subsequently published after her death in 'Through England on a Side Saddle' (1888) and are available at www.visionofbritain.org.uk. Owned by Tennants Brewery, the pub eventually closed in 1952 and the licence was transferred to a nearby pub, the Mossbrook. The premises are still standing as two whitewashed cottages that stand at right angles to the main road, at the bottom of Beighton Hill. The Coach & Horses is one of several Eckington pubs mentioned in the words of an Eckington drinking song called, 'The Running Gill', which were kindly supplied by Bernard Clegg:

> **The Running Gill**
> *The Bear can beat the Duke and Prince*
> *And make the Angels fly*
> *To turn the Coach & Horses round*
> *And sup the White Hart dry.*

Lion & Lamb   *High Street*

Whilst this pub was first recorded in an 1849 Trade Directory, the building is probably older and may have been converted into a pub. Previous owners included Brampton Brewery and Sheffield Free Brewery (1930s). Following closure in early 2001, the building remained empty and derelict for several years before demolition in March 2008.

Miners' Arms   *Pitt Street*

The Miners' Arms was originally a beerhouse on Pitt Street that can be dated back to the early 1870s. John Hague is first listed as being licensee of the Miners' Arms in 1883, but was first mentioned as running a beerhouse in Eckington in 1872. It is a fair assumption then that the Miners' Arms opened about this time. Hague was last listed in a Trade Directory in 1883. Other early licensees were James Newton (1887-1888) and Edward Armston (1893-1902). A full licence was not granted until 1949. Owned by Tomlinson's Brewery of Sheffield ('Anchor Beers'), following a merger in 1944, the pub became a Hope & Anchor Brewery tied house, and was eventually absorbed into the Bass empire. The pub closed in January 2001, re-opening on 9th November 2001 as 'Haigh's', only to close for good, circa 2002/3.

White Hart   *Church Street*

Believed to date back to the era of King Richard II, whose badge was a white hart or male deer, it occupied a prime position next to the 12th century parish church. Unusually, the pub continued to brew its own beer into the 20th century. The brewhouse was situated at the rear of the pub and built as early as the 14th century; an age based on expert examination of the stone lintels used in its construction. In the 1920s the

White Hart seen in 2000 shortly after closure.

owners, the Merrymans, sold up and the pub came under brewery ownership.

Many Eckington residents still fondly recall the quality of the Home Brewery beers that were subsequently available in the pub. Mick Jagger, who has family connections in Eckington, visited the pub in the late 1990s, but the landlady was quoted as saying that he didn't offer to pay for his drink!

The doors of this historic inn closed for the last time in 1999 - reflecting the harsh fact that Eckington had too many pubs (or not enough drinkers). A planning application was approved in August 2000 and the pub building was converted to flats. Its associated outbuildings including the remains of that historic brewhouse were demolished, although the stone lintels mentioned above were saved. However, it is to no one's credit that part of Derbyshire's heritage can get dumped, so easily, in a skip.

The old brew house seen in 2000.

ELMTON

Elm Tree   Spring Lane

This former farm building was first listed as a pub in 1852, while John Jackson was the licensee as well as being a blacksmith. The 'Elm Tree' name is a reference to the trees that used to be abundant in the village and it has been owned by both the Duke of Portland and Worksop & Retford Brewery (in 1953). It is now a freehouse.

Licensing records for 1753 show that the population of Elmton, or at least those who liked a drink, could support two licensed victuallers. Seventy-five years later, Glover's Directory for 1828 listed one pub in Elmton – the 'Plough & Dove'. The connection, if any, between the Elm Tree and Plough & Dove remains one of life's little unsolved mysteries.

HANDLEY

The area under consideration here consists of the village of Middle Handley along with the nearby hamlets of West and Nether Handley. Part of Staveley parish, it was reputed to have been part of an area given to Beauchief Abbey in 1175 by Robert Fitz Ranulph as penance for his involvement in the murder of Thomas Becket. Whatever the exact circumstances of the Abbey acquiring Handley, their lands were seized by Henry VIII during the Dissolution of the Monasteries in the 16th century. Subsequently, Handley was given by the Crown to Sir John Frecheville in 1664, after he had been created a peer. Sir John sold his lands at Staveley to the first Duke of Devonshire in 1681, and subsequently they passed to later Dukes. As a result, a number of local Public Houses are called 'Devonshire Arms'.

Early alehouses

A review of the earliest register of Licensed Victuallers shows the following entries under Handley:

1753 Widow Bate
1760 James Green
1764 George Bate

George Bate had a cottage in Middle Handley, from which the alehouse would have operated. Maureen Lyon and Beth Shaw, in their book 'This Remote Township', also state that there was an alehouse in 1689 at West Handley in what is now Orchard Cottage, the evidence being an excise duty payment made by the proprietor, John Rogers.

By the 19th century, the site of the local alehouse had moved again, and it was now found at Parkgate Farm, near Nether Handley. In 'This Remote Township' the authors suggest that the quantity of accommodation for horses tends to support the idea that Parkgate was not only a farm, but also offered facilities for travellers. White's 1833 Trade Directory lists this beerhouse as being run by Isaac Bagshaw. There is no reference to it from 1841 onwards although by this time another beerhouse had opened by at Middle Handley.

Devonshire Arms   *Westfield Lane*

The Devonshire pictured in 2007 following refurbishment. [Nick Wheat]

Benjamin Rodgers was first recorded as running a beerhouse at Middle Handley in White's 1841 Trade Directory. From 1857, this un-named beerhouse had developed into a fully licensed public house, known as the 'Devonshire Arms'. Rodgers was also a farmer, renting 17 acres of land from the Duke of Devonshire, and would have sold beer from the farmhouse to provide himself with extra income. The farmhouse, said to have been built in the 16th or 17th century, stood on the site of the current pub until it was demolished in 1869 and the current premises were built.

The original alehouse/farmhouse was recorded for posterity in a painting by John Cowley (see 'This Remote Township', page 77). The artist was also the landlord of the pub, having taken over after Benjamin Rodgers' death in 1864. Accordingly John Cowley was the first landlord of the new Devonshire Arms.

Until the 20th century the pub was still part of a working farm. An inventory taken in 1889, when John Cowley died, included farm buildings that consisted of a stable, cowhouse for six cows, pigsties, a turnip house, a barn and two sheds. The next licensee was Frederick (known as 'Fred') Marples from Eckington, who was also recorded as being a farmer in Bulmer's 1895 Trade Directory. By 1905 the farm had 58 acres of land.

In 1924 Fred risked his life to save a young woman and child from drowning in a well at Marsh Quarry – his bravery was covered in the local newspaper and was recognized by the Royal Humane Society. However, Fred's own life ended in tragic circumstances in the early 1930s when he committed suicide. The pub's licence was taken over by his wife, and then by his son, Bernard, who bought the pub and farm buildings from the Duke of Devonshire in 1954. Bernard left the pub around 1959. The licence was then held briefly by Bill Richardson (1959-60) until Tom and Jean Walker took over as tenants in August 1960, by which time the pub had been acquired by William Stones Brewery of Sheffield. Tom and Jean ran it as a traditional village local serving good quality beer, which ensured that the 'Dev' appeared several times in CAMRA's Good Beer Guide. So it must have come as a shock in 1994 when they were shown a newspaper article by a customer announcing that the Devonshire was to be sold and converted into a topless fun bar – subsequently, their concerns proved to be groundless as the newspaper was dated 1st April and was not the genuine thing …..!

Tom and Jean eventually bought the pub back from William Stones and remained at the pub for over 44 years until Tom's death in early 2005. It is very likely that they were the longest serving landlord and landlady in any North Derbyshire pub at this time.

The Devonshire remained shut for almost two years and indeed there were significant fears that it might never re-open and instead be converted to a house. Fortunately it was eventually bought by two local businessmen, Glen Saint and Craig Jackson, and, following refurbishment, the 'Dev' opened its doors again on 23rd December 2006. It retains the atmosphere of a traditional village local and features beers from local breweries.

'Refurbished Devonshire interior, December 2007

Finally, there is a more gruesome side to the history of the pub for in April 1873 it had featured in a local murder. The body of the victim, Eliza Hudson, was laid out on a table in the pub for an initial examination and subsequent post mortem undertaken by a local doctor. The murderer, Eliza's estranged husband Ben, was quickly caught and subsequently executed at Derby.

HIGHAM

Higham is said to mean 'high village' from the old English 'heah' and 'ham'. Situated between Clay Cross and Alfreton, its main street follows the line of Ryknield Street, built by the Romans. However, there is no evidence of any sort of settlement at this time and it is not mentioned in the Domesday Book, but neighbouring Shirland is. So we don't know for certain when a formal settlement first developed. If we move forward in time by 150 years or so, a village had developed and in 1243 Higham was granted the right to hold a weekly market and an annual fair, the latter to be held between 31st July and 2nd August. Higham's prosperity was primarily due to its position on the main route between Sheffield and Derby. However, this changed in 1792, when a turnpike road was constructed and travellers were diverted through Shirland and onto Alfreton, leading to a sharp decline in Higham's fortunes during the 19th century. Today, most traffic continues on the A61 towards Shirland and Alfreton, ensuring that there is a peaceful environment in which to enjoy Higham's charms. These include a main street lined with 17th century houses (some are even older), three public houses and a restored market cross that sits on its original steps.

Black Bull   *Main Road*

The premises that were formerly the Black Bull Inn and are now known as Bull Farm can be dated back with certainty to the 15th century. Having said that, the experts also state that two internal timber cruck frames come from the late-medieval period. So, if nothing else, this must be one of the oldest buildings in the village and a date stone of 1673 is a red herring, included during later alterations. A Department of Environment survey has concluded that the building was altered a number of times, between the 18th and 20th centuries. It is now a Grade 2 listed building.

Records indicate that it was operating as an inn by 1724 and it is likely that it was one of the two alehouses known to have existed in Higham in 1577. By the 18th century the Black Bull was Higham's main inn, evidenced by the fact that it hosted manor courts. There are also records of theatrical performances held at the pub by travelling players in the late 18th century. Indeed, it is said that the inn had its own ballroom and temporary theatre. Stagecoaches also used the inn until the new turnpike road was opened. The inn closed circa 1877, evidencing Higham's declining fortunes in the 19th century.

Barley Mow/Crown *Main Road*
Built as four cottages in the 18th century, which were completely re-fronted in the early 19th century, this pub was originally known as the Barley Mow. An 1851 plan shows a complex that included a dwelling house, farm buildings and a malt house, the latter being evidence that the pub may have brewed its own beer at some time. The name change to the Crown took place between 1880 and 1881.

In the late 19th century the pub was owned or leased by Hollis' Willow Tree Brewery of Pilsley, which ceased brewing circa 1914. The pub lease was subsequently taken over by Chesterfield Brewery and then Mansfield Brewery, the latter eventually buying the whole of the former Hollis pub estate in 1944.

The Crown is still open and is situated towards the Alfreton (South) end of Main Road, with car parking at the rear. The pub has a marriage licence, allowing civil weddings to take place there.

Greyhound *Main Road*
Trade Directories confirm that the Greyhound was open in 1821 when the licensee was James Widdowson. Records also show that the building was part of a 42-acre holding, which was altered and extended in 1835. The pub's position, at the Northern end of the village, meant that it remained on the main route after the new turnpike road was built. Having been owned by Gilmours Brewery of Sheffield for a period, it is now owned by Marston's Pub Company, has been greatly extended and is a busy roadside pub.

Higham Farm Hotel *Main Road*
A hotel with public bar, created from the modernisation and conversion of Higham Farm in the 1970s. Known as Santo's Higham Farm Hotel, it is one of three Public Houses that remain open in the village.

Horns *Main Road (formerly High Street)*
Situated at 27-28 High Street, next to the 19th century market cross (which replaced an earlier one of circa 1753), the Horns closed sometime around 1860/1. Known licensees include John Swain (1814) and John Wharton (1823). Use of the name 'Horns' suggests that the pub aimed to get its trade from the stagecoaches that once passed through Higham – one of the coach driving team would sound a horn to warn the landlord that their arrival was imminent.

Plough *Main Road (formerly High Street)*
The farmhouse buildings known as 'Well Farm,' situated across the road and along from the Greyhound, were built at various stages between the 15th and 20th centuries according to a survey by the Department of Environment. Records also show that in 1772 the farm included an "alehouse and shop" occupied by John Osgathorpe. In 1814 it was described as a "Public House, yard, garden, wood-yard, and wheelwright's shop" and the licensee in 1835, Samuel Cheetham, also traded as a wheelwright to supplement his income from the pub. The pub closed sometime during the period 1842-46.

The former Plough in 2005.

Three Stags' Heads
Main Road (formerly High Street)

It is believed that the premises were rebuilt in the 18th century by the Towndrow family and became a Public House around that time. The Three Stags' Heads had closed by 1821 - an early casualty of Higham's 19th century decline. The premises are still standing and are now known as Ivy Farm.

The former Three Stags' Heads in 2005.

Beerhouse
An un-named beerhouse is also known to existed in Higham in the 19th century. Situated to the rear of the Crown Inn, it was recorded in 1846 when the licensee was John North.

HOLMESFIELD
In her book, 'All Their Yesterdays', Bessie Bunker describes Holmesfield as: "an Ancient Derbyshire Village on the south-eastern foothills of the Pennines" and she goes on to observe that: "It is a village of hamlets, of which Holmesfield is the focus, and which, quite rightly, has given its name to the whole parish." The only thing I would add is that Holmesfield is just far enough away from Dronfield to give it both independence and a sense of tranquillity.

Angel Inn
Main Road

Generally accepted, by some margin, as being the oldest pub in Holmesfield. The fact that it occupies a prime position, near the church, gives credence to the suggestion that it was originally a brewhouse supplying church officials, also offering accommodation to guests of the church from the 16th century onwards. Indeed, the pub was owned by the church until the 1950s and in 1953 was leased by the Vicar of Holmesfield to John Smith's Brewery. Regrettably, the new owners demolished these historic buildings and erected a new pub, which still stands today.

The original Angel Inn c.1920. [Bob Gratton collection]

George & Dragon
Main Road

This former farmhouse has been extended and converted over time to become the present day pub. It is one of two Holmesfield pubs listed in early 19th century Trade Directory records, the other being the Angel. The George & Dragon was acquired from private ownership by Duncan Gilmour & Co. of Sheffield in 1934.

Horns Inn
Main Road

The Horns Inn was originally a beerhouse that did not appear in records before 1846. Past owners include two Sheffield Breweries - Thomas Berry and then Tennant's. A long-serving 20th century landlord was Ron Barton who took over the pub in 1952 and did not leave until the early 1990s. It is still open.

Peacock   *Owler Bar*

It is thought that the original pub may have opened around the same time as the nearby tollbars, which date from the second half of the 18th century. However, to date, it has not proved possible to substantiate this with other records. At some stage the original building was replaced by the current premises, probably in the 19th century. The name comes from the fact that the pub was built on land owned by the Duke of Rutland, whose family crest was a peacock.

Robin Hood   *Lydgate*

A former farmhouse, the Robin Hood was a rare Inde Coope Brewery outlet in North Derbyshire, although ownership had passed to Brampton Brewery by the 1950s. It closed around 2002 and was sold for residential development.

The Robin Hood c.1953.
[Holmesfield Village Society collection]

Rutland Arms   *Cowley Bar*

The date that this Wards Brewery beerhouse opened is not known. As it originally held a beerhouse licence, it must have opened sometime during the period 1830-70 and it is likely that a beerhouse at Cowley, listed in an 1857 directory, was the Rutland. It remains open for business.

Travellers Rest   *Main Road*

This is another beerhouse where the opening date has been difficult to pin down precisely. There was an un-named beerhouse listed in an 1833 Trade Directory, at Holmesfield, which could have been either the Travellers or Horns. Previous owners include John Smith's and Home Breweries. The pub was the birthplace of the Sheffield branch of the CAMRA, the Campaign for Real Ale in 1974; they are still waiting for the blue heritage plaque to be put up..... Whilst the public bar is still open, most custom comes from the Thai restaurant also on the premises and it is now known as 'Thai at the Travellers'.

Un-named beerhouse   *Fox Lane*

Local hearsay has it that there was a small beerhouse on Fox Lane, possibly connected with a farm. It hasn't proved possible to verify this to date from formal records, although that is not to say it didn't exist at some stage.

MARSH LANE

Marsh Lane was probably little more than a collection of farms and smallholdings until the late 18th century. Its importance always lagged behind its near neighbours such as Eckington, Troway and Ridgeway, which all had industries such as scythe and sickle making to bring greater prosperity. However, the construction of the Eckington to Coal Aston turnpike in the 1790s brought with it the need to service the requirements of travellers. With a growing population, this resulted in a total of four pubs and beerhouses opening by the mid-1860s, of which only one is still open.

Butchers' Arms   *Main Road*

The first evidence of the Butcher's Arms (and the source of the pub's name) is as an un-named beerhouse listed in 1833. The licensee, Charles Booth, was also listed as a butcher. For many years Brampton Brewery owned the pub. It was closed as this book went to press.

Fox & Hounds   Main Road

A pub that was first listed in an 1833 Trade Directory when the victualler was Luke White. It is thought that the building was originally farm cottages, and that the pub was created from the conversion of two cottages in the late 18th /early 19th century. Indeed, two former doorways are visible at the front of the property. This could have occurred in the 1790s when the turnpike road, linking Eckington and Coal Aston, was constructed. To attract passing trade from the turnpike road, the pub had small safes built into a wall where travellers could keep their valuables. The pub was extended after the Second World War, the evidence is still visible from the outside, and the most recent alterations took place in 2000 when it underwent a £250,000 refurbishment. Chesterfield, Mansfield and Burtonwood Breweries have all owned the pub, which is now part of Marston's Pub Company.

George   Lightwood Road

Opened in the 1850s, the George was originally owned by Worksop & Retford Brewery, but by the 1990s it had become a popular free house and a regular entry in CAMRA's Good Beer Guide. The fortunes of the pub then took a downturn, and planning permission was requested for the pub to be replaced by a housing development, initially in late 2002. The George Inn closed its doors for the last time on Sunday 24th November 2002, and with the necessary planning permission finally obtained in April 2003, the pub was demolished in May 2003. George IV, who reigned 1820-30, was depicted on the last signboard.

Prince of Wales   Lightwood Road

A beerhouse that was situated at 54 Lightwood Road, just along from the George, and is thought to have originally brewed its own beer. Later on it was owned or leased by Sheffield Free Brewery, famous for their 'Matchless Ales'. A notable statistic from the pub's history is that the licensees for the whole of the period 1862-1921 were both called William Ridgeway, and were father and son. As well as running the beerhouse, William senior also worked as a coal miner in order to keep his wife and four children plus a house servant. After closure around 1960, the premises stood derelict for several years until sold by auction in 1971 as a private residence.

The derelict Prince of Wales in April 1966.

Fortunately photographic evidence of the Prince of Wales remains – in particular a Harvest Festival scene featuring landlord and landlady Fred and Annie Rollins, and their daughter Mary. Turning to the source of the name, the Prince of Wales opened in the early 1860s, and like many new pubs from around that time, was named after the hugely popular eldest son of Queen Victoria, who eventually succeeded her as Edward VII in 1901, and reigned until his own death in 1910.

Harvest Festival at the Prince of Wales showing landlord and landlady, Fred and Annie Rollins and their daughter Mary.

Past and Present 45

NEW WHITTINGTON

Originally a farming community and part of Whittington, the area now known as New Whittington developed following the opening in 1857 of Messrs Thomas Firth & Sons Ironworks. At one time it could support eleven pubs; five of these remain open today and two of the ex-pubs now earn their keep as residential properties.

Angel   *South Street North*

First listed as a public house in 1868, the Angel was once one of the three pubs or beerhouses that stood on South Street North, the others being the Bull's Head and Star Inn, and is the only one still open. Originally the pub was owned by Tennant Brothers' Brewery of Sheffield who became part of Whitbread in 1961/2.

Bath Hotel   *London Street*

The Bath Hotel, situated on London Street, was a Scarsdale Brewery beerhouse that was initially known as the 'Plough' (1869-1891). The hotel was demolished in the mid 1980s and the land was used as a car park for the nearby school. We can get a good idea of the pub's layout from plans submitted in December 1935. These show that the building adjoined the Co-operative Shop premises and that there was an upstairs club room. Further plans to enlarge the tap room and add a ladies toilet were approved in February 1962.

Bull's Head   *South Street North*

The Bull's Head, on South Street North, was converted into a beerhouse around 1868. Richdale's and Hammond's Breweries have both owned the pub over the years. It closed in the late 1960s. The property, now converted into flats, stands just down the road from the Angel.

The former Bull's Head premises 2000.

Crown Inn/Corner Flag   *High Street*

The Crown Inn, so named because it was built on land known as 'Crown Yard', was first listed in 1862 as a beerhouse. Plans submitted in 1917 show that it had a bar parlour and smoke room on the left, with a 'General Room' on the right. Chesterfield and Mansfield Breweries have both been owners. In summer 2001 it was purchased by Innspire Pub Group and renamed as the Corner Flag – a sporting theme pub. It was closed as this book went to press.

Dusty Miller   *High Street*

The 'Dusty Miller Yard' seen in the 1930s. The beerhouse is on the left, although only part of it can be seen. The middle building (with outside steps) is thought to have been the old malt house. The long building on the right is the rear of a terrace of four houses (Nos. 104-110) which fronted onto High Street.
[John Hirst collection]

The most interesting of all the 'lost' New Whittington pubs is the Dusty Miller. The first evidence of this beerhouse is under the name of the 'Malt Shovel' in 1857. The licensee, John Hollingworth, bought a malt house premises in 1855 for £420. In 1874, the death certificate for one Joseph Cundy listed his occupation as a beerhouse keeper, address 'Dusty Miller'. The premises were situated in a yard off High Street, hidden from view from the road by a terrace of four dwelling houses, whilst the name originates from the fact that an early landlord was from a milling family. It is likely that beer was brewed on the premises until two Sheffield brewers, John Akenhead and Barton Wells, bought the business for £1010 in December 1889. Ownership later passed to Greaves Brewery of Sheffield until 1920 when Greaves were taken over by another Sheffield Brewer, Duncan Gilmour & Co. The Dusty Miller closed around 1922 when objections were made to the renewal of its licence. The premises, together with the adjoining malt house and terraced houses, were eventually demolished in the late 1930s. Four houses next to 'Cheers' Off Licence on High Street, and part of Highgate Close to the rear, now occupy the site.

Forge Inn   Station Lane
Originally a beerhouse that opened about 1859, the Forge Inn takes its name from Firth's ironworks that were once found nearby. Truswells Brewery of Sheffield owned the pub until 1955 when they were taken over by Hope & Anchor (in due course acquired by Bass).

Miners' Arms   Bamford Street
The oldest surviving public house in New Whittington is the Miners' Arms on Bamford Street, having first been listed in an 1857 Trade Directory. The probable source of the name is from the fact that an early landlord, George Bamford, was also a miner and no doubt he wanted to attract the custom of his fellow miners. The pub has been owned by Chesterfield Brewery, Mansfield Brewery (from 1938), and Burtonwood Brewery and Wolverhampton & Dudley Breweries. The latter became Marston's Pub Company in 2006.

Rising Sun   High Street
The Rising Sun was another pub in the village that was owned by Scarsdale Brewery of Chesterfield. This end-terrace pub opened in the late 1860s and until 1960 only held a beerhouse licence.

Royal Hotel   London Street
The Royal Hotel started life as a beerhouse called the Royal Oak in the 1860s also on London Street. This Brampton Brewery outlet closed in 1958 and the premises were demolished in 1972/3.

Star Inn   South Street North
Another beerhouse, on South Street North, was the Star Inn. Owned by Scarsdale Brewery, it was closed in 1959 under the 1904 Licensing Act. This was the so-called 'Compensation Act', which allowed local magistrates to close pubs and beerhouses in areas where they felt there were too many, in return for a compensation payment. The property still stands and is the pebble dashed house next to the Angel.

Wellington Hotel   High Street
Situated on High Street, the Wellington Hotel was built as a hotel/pub in 1858, a fact confirmed by a date stone at the side of the pub. At one time there was a stable block for horses at the rear. The first known landlord was a John Wilcockson (1858-68). Yet again, both Chesterfield and Mansfield Breweries have been owners and it is now part of Marston's Pub Company. The pub has developed a reputation for serving fine real ales over the last few years, earning it an entry in the Good Beer Guide.

OLD WHITTINGTON

Until the mid-19th century the whole of this area was just plain 'Whittington', the 'Old' being added to give the original community a separate identity from 'New' Whittington, which appeared in the 1850s. Nine inns and pubs are known to have existed of which four are still open.

Bulls Head — Broomhill Road

The Bulls Head has origins as an old alehouse that dated back to the 17th century, maybe earlier. The original stone building was demolished in 1907, and rebuilt as a pub/hotel by the owners Brampton Brewery. Since 1962, the pub has been owned by John Smiths Brewery, which ultimately became the owner of Brampton Brewery pubs. Between 1821 and 1870, the licensees were a John Cooke and then Hannah Cooke, who were probably husband and wife. John Cooke was also a blacksmith.

Cock & Magpie — Church Street North

The Cock & Magpie was built to replace the historic Cock & Pynot inn, which still stands in front of it, and 'Pynot' is an old Derbyshire word for magpie. The old alehouse played a key role in English history. In 1688 a group of local Protestant noblemen, seeking to avoid a rainstorm, ended up here to plan their part in the 'Glorious Revolution'. As a result of the plans they made, King James II, a Catholic, was deposed and replaced by the Protestant William of Orange and his queen, Mary. The alehouse was open for another 100 years after the Revolution, until the Cock & Magpie was built in 1790. Mansfield Brewery owned the new pub over the period 1935-2000, prior to that it belonged to Chesterfield Brewery. It is now part of Marston's Pub Company.

Cock & Magpie with the former Cock & Pynot (now known as Revolution House) in the foreground 2002.

Compass — High Street

Records show that the Compass, also referred to as the Square & Compass, was open in 1821 and that it closed during the period 1849-1852. The only known licensee, George Bower, is also listed as being a cattle dealer and a farmer at 'Compass Farm', and the pub undoubtedly operated from the farm buildings that stood on High Street. The farm was pulled down many years ago and the site used for a petrol station, although this too was subsequently demolished and the land is now a housing development. As a reminder of what once existed, streets named Compass Crescent and Bower Farm Road can still be found.

Newbridge Inn — Foxley Oakes

The Newbridge Inn was situated in an area known as Foxley Oakes and was first listed in 1870 when the landlord was John Wilcox, who was also a shoemaker. In 1912 the pub was leased to John Smiths Brewery but it closed in 1914.

Pheasant Inn — The Brushes

The Pheasant Inn was situated in a terraced row along from the Railway. The beerhouse, which was known to have been open in 1869 and was owned by Brampton Brewery, had a relatively short life and closed in 1907 under the Compensation Act. The terraced row is still standing, albeit some of the properties are in need of urgent repair.

Poplar Inn — Church Street North

Until it closed in 2003, the Poplar Inn could be found hidden away in quiet surroundings on Church Street North. The premises were originally a private house built during the period 1700-50. About 1870 the house was bought by a Nottinghamshire miner, named John Bamford, who converted part of the building for use as a beerhouse. Subsequently, Chesterfield Brewery bought the beerhouse and a full licence was granted in 1951. The pub took its name from a large house that stood opposite the pub, which was known as the 'Poplars' on account of the poplar trees in its garden. It is now a private house.

The Poplar seen in 2002 before closure. [Nick Wheat]

Railway — The Brushes

A pub that has had several names is the Railway, one of the three pubs once found in an area that is still known as 'The Brushes'. It was originally a beerhouse known as the Railway Inn, which first traded around 1868, coinciding with the opening of the new Sheffield-Chesterfield railway. Situated at 148 Sheffield Road, just off today's busy A61 bypass, it was handily placed for the massive Sheepbridge steelworks. Beers were supplied by John Smiths brewery. Older readers may recall that the sign affixed to the pub's wall showed George Stephenson's 'Rocket'. The name was changed to the Two Jays in the 1980s, the inspiration being the initials of the two people who owned the pub at that time. There was a further name change to the Odd Couple during the 1990s, before it reverted to its original name in 2006.

Sheepbridge Hotel — Sheffield Road

The Sheepbridge Hotel premises are still situated just off the original Sheffield Road and very close to the A61 bypass that is the main route into Sheffield for 21st century travellers. Records indicate that it opened in the 1820s and was probably built as a coaching inn for 19th century travellers on the Sheffield to Chesterfield road. However, this source

Helen Frances

of business dried up when the railway link arrived in the late 1860s. The pub, which was owned for many years by Richdales Brewery of Sheffield, closed in January 1978. The premises are now used as offices, although etched windows from its time as a pub are still visible.

DEMOLISHED EARLY 2012

The Swan

RIDGEWAY

Follow me: @

Two men with links to Sheffield that have gone on trial accused of terrorism offences were attempting to manufacture a device that would allow them to detonate explosives in a driverless car, a court heard.

During the opening of the trial yesterday, jurors heard how Sheffield resident, Farhad Salah, told a contact in December last year that he was attempting to find a way to

White Horse — *High Street*

The White Horse was built as, or converted into, a pub around 1780 to provide accommodation and refreshments to travellers on the road from Chesterfield to Rotherham. The name is derived from the emblem of Germany's House of Hanover, one of their mob (mad King George III) being king when the inn opened. The pub was rebuilt during the 20th century and now has a mock Tudor frontage. At some point the White Horse was purchased by Tennant's Brewery of Sheffield, who merged with Whitbread in 1961-2. It is now owned by Enterprise Inns, and makes use of Enterprise's scheme that allows it to source some of its real ales from local microbreweries.

RIDGEWAY

Historically included in the Marsh Lane district for licensing purposes.

Bridge Inn — *The Ford*

Became licensed premises in the 1840s (a beerhouse is listed in Trade Directories at Ford as early as 1842, the licensee being Isaac Guest). In 1849 Isaac Guest was still at the pub, which now had a full licence (rather than the more easily obtainable beerhouse licence). Brewery owners have included A H Smith, Tennants and Thwaites. An engraved stone built into the front wall of the pub states: 'The Land Tax of all the Buildings belonging to J Hutton in this Parish is redeemed 1823'. The Hutton's were a Ridgeway family with scythe-making interests and may have owned the Bridge before it was an inn. The pub is well situated for exploring the nearby woods, in which can be found the restored 'Seldom Seen Engine House'. The Engine House is thought to have been built between 1855 and 1875 and once housed a massive winding wheel for Plumbley Colliery. The Penny Engine Railway (so named because the fare was one old penny) ran from here to Renishaw.

Phoenix — *High Lane*

Still open, and originally near to the works of T.J. Hutton, who exported scythes and sickles all over the world. The works, which opened in 1822, eventually became known as the Phoenix Scythe works, and the pub may have opened about the same time to get the custom of the 20 people employed there. It may have taken a while for sufficient trade to be built up as a landlord in the 1820s, Robert Turner, was also a carpenter. Brewery owners have included John Smiths and Sheffield Free Brewery.

SUTTON CUM DUCKMANTON

The parish of Sutton cum Duckmanton arose out of the 16th century merger of two smaller parishes, Sutton and Duckmanton, and indeed several separate settlements still exist in the enlarged parish. Duckmanton has historically consisted of the village of Long Duckmanton, and the hamlets of Middle and Far Duckmanton, while Sutton Scarsdale is home to the historic Sutton Scarsdale Hall, rebuilt in 1724 on the site of an earlier 15th century building.

The development and prosperity of the parish has been partly tied to the fortunes, whims and fancies of the Arkwright family, with a little help from coal. In the 1880s, the Arkwright family leased the coal rights for their land to Staveley Coal & Iron Company. Arkwright Town was subsequently built to house the miners.

Duckmanton Hotel — *Tom Lane*

Known locally as "Top Duck", the Duckmanton Hotel was built in 1928 by Chesterfield Brewery and subsequently it became a Mansfield Brewery house, until ownership passed to Cameron's in the late 1980s. The first landlord was William Wells.

Arkwright Arms — Chesterfield Road

Helen Frances

To understand the history of the Arkwright Arms, we first have to look into the fate of the White Swan, a pub that used to stand on the same piece of land (although closer to the road). The White Swan was an old alehouse, dating back to the 18th century, maybe earlier. One theory is that it opened to serve travellers on the old London to York road, which passed through the village. The pub closed when its licence was not renewed in 1871. Mrs Arkwright, mother of William Arkwright, apparently ordered the pub's closure on suspicion that the local poachers were meeting there, and it remained closed until the old lady died, 14 years later, in 1885. As William Arkwright, a descendant of the inventor Richard Arkwright, enabled the pub to re-open, it was re-named 'Arkwright's Arms' in his honour. The name was amended later to the Arkwright Arms. In February 1927, alterations to the pub were approved and owners Brampton Brewery rebuilt it. The Arkwright, known locally as 'Bottom Duck', remains a lively pub and has picked up a number of awards from the Chesterfield Branch of CAMRA including their 2008 'Pub of the Year' award.

Poolsbrook Hotel — Cottage Close

The Poolsbrook Hotel should also be mentioned as it also falls just inside the parish. Built in 1892, this pub remains open today and stands at the southern tip of Poolsbrook village.

Prince of Wales — No location

The tale of the Prince of Wales is about a pub that was named, but never built. In February 1927, the Brampton Brewery Company withdrew an application for a licence for a new pub at Duckmanton. It would appear that this change of heart was as a result of approval being given to the proposed alterations to the Arkwright Arms. This theory ties in with the fact that in June 1934 Brampton Brewery auctioned a "piece of old grass land having a frontage of about 95 feet to the road from Chesterfield to Bolsover at Duckmanton (near to Robertson Avenue)". As part of the condition of sale, the vendor had to agree not to use the land for a hotel or public house, or for brewing. This land was probably acquired as a site for the new pub that the Brewery would have erected if they had not been allowed to rebuild the Arkwright Arms.

Rose & Crown — Location not known

Little evidence of one pub, the Rose & Crown, exists. Licensing records show that there were originally two licensed victuallers in the parish, and that a William Sales held a licence as early as 1820. The pub is listed only in an 1835 trade directory when the landlord was John Sales.

Station Hotel — Arkwright Town

Station Hotel. [John Hirst collection]

Opened in March 1903, the Station Hotel at Arkwright Town was another Brampton Brewery house. Although William Arkwright had applied for the licence, the licensing report records that there was a legal technicality preventing him owning pubs on his land. To overcome this, William Arkwright placed the Arkwright Arms and Station Hotel under the Staveley District Public House Trust Co, whose object was to promote temperance. The pub closed around 1995 when residents were forced to leave 'old' Arkwright Town, due to a methane gas problem, and move across the road to new Arkwright Town.

White Swan — Chesterfield Road

A group photograph taken outside the White Swan. [John Chadwick collection]

The oldest known pub in the area, the White Swan was situated where the Arkwright Arms is today. See the 'Arkwright Arms' entry for further details.

TADDINGTON

The historic settlement of Taddington, situated between Buxton and Bakewell, benefited in the 18th century from stone quarrying and lead mining, which took place nearby. As early as 1760, three licensed victuallers were recorded in the village, and further trade from stagecoach travellers came after the Buxton to Ashford turnpike road, which passed through Taddington, was completed in 1810. Indeed, it was not until the middle of the 20th century that a by-pass was built to take traffic on the busy A6 main road away from the village.

In total six different inns, pubs or beerhouses are known to have existed. The Queens' Arms and the Waterloo (outside of the main village on the A6) are still open, while three of the former public houses are still standing.

Bull's Head — Main Road

Records show that the pub was open in the first half of the 19th century and that it had closed by 1851. The landlord in 1827 was John Schofield. The Bull's Head is believed to have stood in the centre of the village opposite the Queens' Arms, although the building was demolished long ago.

George Inn — Main Road

Licensing records show that the George Inn (or hotel) was open in the 1750s and continued to offer refreshment to both locals and travellers until ordered to close for Compensation in August 1958. It held a full licence, and was owned by Offilers Brewery. The property still stands, and is the first building reached, at the junction of Main Road and Waterlees Road, when approaching the village from Bakewell. The landlord in 1827 was Thomas Maycock.

Miners' Arms/Queen's Arms — Main Road

The Queen's Arms (pictured centre) seen from afar in 2003. [Nathan Gale]

This old inn dates back to 1736, although it was used as a farmhouse before that. For many years in the 1700s the Miners' Arms was run by the Orme family, and it has also been owned both by Chesterfield Brewery (1870s) and Hill's Cromford Brewery (1880s). The cellar has also been used as a morgue, although it appears that this was mainly for the convenience of the local coffin-maker, who was based across the road! The name was changed to the Queen's Arms to mark the occasion of Queen Victoria's Golden Jubilee in 1887. It was also tacit acknowledgement of the decline in importance of lead mining in the locality by the end of the 19th century, and the landlord decided instead to show his support for the reigning monarch.

Star Inn — Main Road

The former Star Inn still stands at the western end of the village next to the church, and is now a private residence known as 'Star House'. Whilst little information has come to light about the pub, it is known that the landlord in 1827 was George Hibbert, and that it was ordered to close for Compensation in June 1916. It is not known which brewery supplied beer to the pub. Taddington Church has a stone font that was once used for washing beer mugs in the Star Inn (see later).

Travellers Rest — Main Road
Records confirm that this beerhouse was in existence in 1857, and that it was ordered to close for Compensation in June 1910. The last known landlord was Samuel Bennett jnr. The building is now a bed and breakfast establishment known as 'Marlborough House', and it stands at the western end of the village (on the opposite side of the road to the Queen's Arms).

Waterloo Inn — A6
Originally known as 'Waterloo House', this Robinson's pub is situated next to the A6 main road to the west of the village. It was first recorded as being open in 1846 when the landlord was Anthony Mason.

The stone font in Taddington Church

J Charles Cox, in a book called 'Notes on Derbyshire Churches', gives the following information on a font that he found in the Star Inn at Taddington. "Fixed to the wall, to the left of the fire-place and supported in a stone with notched edges is what we suppose to be the circular bowl of a former font, of the Norman period". It is not known when and why the font was moved from the church to the Star Inn, but it is said that, amongst other things, it was used for washing beer mugs. In September 1939 this ancient font, which could now be almost 1000 years old, was rescued and returned to Taddington Church, where it can now be found.

TROWAY
Troway (meaning either 'the trough' or 'valley road') lies just beyond Marsh Lane, near Eckington in the Moss Valley. It is a wonderful place for nature and walking, and is possibly North East Derbyshire's best kept secret. From the 15th to the 19th century the area was famed for scythe and sickle production, but the dams and mill wheels are now abandoned or gone. Most of the land is now used for agriculture, and it is easy to forget that the hamlet is little more than six miles from Sheffield city centre.

Black-a-Moor — Snowdon Lane
The oldest pub in the area is now known as the Black-a-moor, but this is a corruption of the pub's original name, the Blackmoor's Head, as recorded in a 19th century Trade Directory. The name is said to have originated from the time of the crusades in the 11th and 12th centuries, when coloured men were regarded as infidel, barbaric and cruel, and the Turks or 'Moors' were regarded as the enemies of Christianity. This is a more likely source of the name rather than the pub's proximity to 'Moortop farm'. Indeed, the pub's signboard used to show a dark moorland scene that probably added to the confusion.

No documentary evidence came to light during research to confirm how old the pub may be. However, it is known that there has been an alehouse on the site for several hundred years, and Ordnance Survey maps confirm that the original premises, which were demolished in the 1930s, stood at right angles to the current building (i.e. facing the road down to Troway). The first known landlord was John Boot (1828). A longstanding 20th century landlord was Ernest Whitworth. The pub was rebuilt in the 1930s by William Stones's brewery in mock Tudor fashion. Indeed, it was one of three Stones pubs locally built at the same time in this style, the other two being the Mason's Arms on Cemetery Road, Dronfield, and the Hearts of Oak, Northern Common, Dronfield Woodhouse. The Black-a-moor is now owned by Enterprise Inns and in April 2008 it was announced that BrewKitchen, the Sheffield gastro-pub company, were to take over the lease and that the pub's name would be changed to "something more politically correct".

The pub's unusual position, apparently in the middle of nowhere, may be explained by the fact that an old trackway passed by it, one of a number in the area. These trackways formed the transport network before the nearby turnpike road was built, allowing people, animals and goods to be moved. When the Black-a-moor was rebuilt in the 1930's, it was said that it was in anticipation of housing development in the surrounding area that never subsequently went ahead. Whereas similar pubs in Dronfield (Mason's Arms) and Dronfield Woodhouse (Hearts of Oak) did eventually become swallowed up by housing development, the Black-a-Moor remains rural.

Gate Inn

Main Road

Helen Frances

The Gate Inn stands just down the hill from the Black-a-moor, on the valley side. The Gate was built as a farmhouse, and cottages for farm workers used to stand where the car park is now. By 1833, part of the property had been given over to a beerhouse, the first recorded landlord being James Oates. It is not known whether beer was ever brewed on the premises, but it is a possibility. The area available to drinkers then was much smaller than it is today, being limited to the front part of today's lounge, a wooden beam marks the point where the beerhouse joined the residential part of the property. The room on the other side, entered from the garden, was not originally part of the beerhouse. In those days, beer was served by jug from the cellar. The beerhouse licence was not replaced with a full licence until 1950.

The 1841 census recorded that James Oates, aged 45, was a beerhouse keeper, and lived with his wife, Elizabeth, also 45 years old, and their children Ann (15 years), Elizabeth (12 years) and Mary (10 years). Again, this suggests that Oates did not have any other occupation and so the beerhouse must have provided enough to live on.

One family with a long association with the Gate is the Allen family. James Allen was listed as running a beerhouse in 1860, and the business subsequently passed to John Allen (who was also a shoemaker), Mary Allen, Alexander Allen and finally, in 1921, Mrs Mary Ellen Allen (probably Alexander's widow). Mary Ellen Allen was still recorded as being at the Gate in 1941.

Several breweries have owned the Gate – Shipstones (early 1900s), Chesterfield Brewery, and then Mansfield Brewery when they acquired Chesterfield Brewery in 1935. Mansfield sold the pub to Burtonwood Brewery in April 1989 in a deal that also included the Fox & Hounds at Marsh Lane. Both pubs are now part of the Marston's pub estate. The Gate hosts a marrow competition every October.

The source of the name the 'Gate' is often proximity to a tollgate on a turnpike road. On this occasion however, it could simply be a reference to a common piece of farming furniture that is very familiar in the Moss Valley – the 5-bar gate (as depicted on the pub's signboard).

Unnamed beerhouse

The opportunity to make a profit from selling beer to Troway's thirsty sickle makers and farm hands attracted competition for a short period. An unnamed beerhouse was listed at Troway in the 1860s, run by Mark Fox. The 1841 census records a Mark Fox living in Troway, at that time he was a 35 year old sickle grinder.

UNSTONE

Situated one mile to the South East of Dronfield, Unstone developed in the 19th century when it started to house miners from the coal mines around Dronfield. Prior to this, another significant development had occurred in the mid 1750s when the turnpike road through the village was constructed. Any existing alehouses would have needed to be expanded in order to handle the extra custom that would have come from travellers, and new licensed premises may also have opened around this time.

Bay Childers   *Main Road*

Said to have been situated next to the Fleur de Lys, the Bay Childers must have closed in the 19th century as it doesn't appear in an 1895 Trade Directory for the area or 20th Century licensing records. This is probably the same pub that is listed as 'Bay Horse' in an 1827/9 Directory, under Dronfield, as there is no other evidence of there being a pub of that name in Dronfield. For the record, the landlord in the 1840s, Joseph Nelson, was also a scissors forger.

Fleur de Lys   *Main Road*

The Fleur de Lys was originally a coaching inn, and took its trade from travellers using the turnpike road that passed next to it. It is not clear if the pub was already in place before construction of the turnpike started around 1756 - possibly it was, and had to be extended and modernised to deal with new trade coming from outside of Unstone. One source (the 1990 CAMRA Derbyshire Ale Guide) states that it stands upon an old wishing well. The licensee in the late 1780/90s was Sarah Parkes, and on her death in 1795 her son Samuel took over the Fleur de Lys until 1821. Moving forward, the pub was owned by Whitmarsh Brewery in the early 1900s, and subsequently was a Gilmours house.

Horse & Groom   *Location not known*

No information has come to light about the Horse & Groom, other than that it had closed by 1895.

Horse & Jockey   *Sheffield Road*

The original Horse & Jockey was located close to where the railway crosses the main road via a bridge at Unstone, and the building still stands at a slight angle to the main road. A Brampton brewery pub, it closed in the 1950s and moved to the current premises at Unstone Green. The first known landlord was Joshua Carnell or Carnally (1827/9). However a 'Joshua Carnelley' is listed as running the 'Black Horse' at Unstone in 1821/2. This is probably the same pub and also evidence that it had been re-named at some time.

The original Horse & Jockey seen in the 1930s.
[George Platts collection]

Let Well be Well   *Highgate Lane*

All the information recorded here comes from Kathleen Battye's book, 'Unstone - the History of a Village' (1980), and it hasn't been possible to verify it against any other sources. Kathleen states that local knowledge has it that there was an alehouse amongst some old cottages on Highgate Lane, now demolished, and the following inscription was just visible on the wall of one of them:

> LET WEL B WELL
> DO H 1648 K WELL
> LOOKE FOOLE AND
> THOU MAY EL AT THE
> MAER NOW GOOS WEL

Nothing else is known about this alehouse, other than it had closed by the early 1820s.

WHITWELL

The historic parish of Whitwell lies close to where the counties of Derbyshire, Yorkshire and Nottinghamshire meet at the 'Shire Oak'. Sherwood Forest once covered the area and the first reference to a settlement at Whitwell was made in 1002. By the 19th century the Duke of Portland was lord of the manor and principal landowner. One of Whitwell's most famous sons was Joe Davis, world snooker champion from the 1920s to the 1940s. His home was on Welbeck Street and it bears a plaque commemorating him.

The number of licensed premises can often be used as an indicator of economic prosperity in an area, and there is a noticeable reduction in the number of public houses in Whitwell towards the end of the 18th century. From a peak of 9 licences in 1764, the number of pubs and inns reduced to 4 by the late 1820's. Things picked up again during the 19th century, and by the 1870s there were 10 licensed premises in the parish.

From Trade Directory records for 1827 we can establish that the two oldest inns in the village centre were the George Inn, later referred to as the Old George Inn, and the Boot & Shoe, which also added the prefix 'Old' to its name for a period as well. Just outside the village, the Half Moon was open in the 1750s.

Bottle & Glass   *Location not known*
During the period 1806-27 trade directories record a pub called the Bottle & Glass. Very little is known about it other than the licensees were William Lindley, James Taylor and Robert Wood. Because of the similarity in names there may be a link with the Jug & Glass.

Boot & Shoe   *High Street*

The Boot & Shoe pictured in 2001

The Boot & Shoe can be traced back to 1753, when John Brownhill was licensee. A Worksop & Retford Brewery house, the pub's name is said to represent the fact that there is a welcome for all comers, whether they wear the horseman's jackboot or the labourer's shoe. The pub, which is still open, can be found in the centre of the village.

Butchers' Arms   *Titchfield Street*
Another Whitwell pub that is still open and situated near the centre of the village, the Butchers' Arms dates back to the 1840s and is so-called because an early landlord, William Marshall, was also a butcher. In 1900 it was bought by Mappin's Brewery of Rotherham, who subsequently merged with William Stones Ltd of Sheffield in 1954.

Dale Inn   *Clinthill Lane*
The Dale Inn, situated at Whitwell Common, was built in 1840, and stands near the scene of a Civil War skirmish. Indeed, a skeleton, ring and sword were found when the pub's foundations were dug. This was yet another former Worksop & Retford Brewery house although, by the time the pub closed in 1994, ownership had passed to Whitbread. It is now a private residence.

George Inn   *High Street*
Situated near the church, the George Inn was an old coaching inn, and once had stabling and harnessing facilities. Some sources state that these were next to the pub, others that the stables were on the other side of the road. Mounting steps, to help people get on their horses, are still visible in front of the building. The earliest known landlord was a Thomas West (1812). A Worksop & Retford Brewery house, it closed in the 1960's, and was converted into flats.

Half Moon — Clinthill Lane

This roadside pub can still be found at Red Hill, just north of the village, on the old Chesterfield to Worksop turnpike road, now the A619. The premises are said to have been built in the 1700s, and their age is best appreciated from the rear of the pub, where there is also a set of derelict stables, possibly used to supply horses for stagecoaches. The first recorded landlord was Samuel Cutts, 1753-67. Once owned by Home Brewery, the pub was part of the Tom Cobleigh chain for many years until the latter were bought by the Spirit Group. It is now branded as a 'Mighty Nice Pub' with a strong emphasis on food.

'Half Moon' was a popular 18th century pub name, often said to be a religious symbol representing the Virgin Mary.

Holmefield Arms — Station Road

First listed as the 'Spirit Vaults' in 1862, but from 1895 onwards it was known more simply as the 'Vaults' or the 'Vaults Hotel' (1951). It was bought from a private owner by Kimberley Brewery, possibly in the 1930s, and then was refurbished, extended and renamed as the Holmefield Arms in the late 1950s. It is an ex- Mansfield Brewery house.

Jug & Glass — Portland Street

Helen Frances

The final pub in the village centre, the Jug & Glass, was first listed in 1846. By the late 19th century, it was owned by the Fox Brewery, of Fox Road, Whitwell. The brewery, which used water from its own spring, was owned, and run, by a Joseph Minkley, and its last brew is said to have taken place in either 1900 or 1901. After the brewery closed, its two pubs, the Jug & Glass and the Royal Oak, Bakestone Moor, were sold to James Hole & Co., brewers of Newark, together with a 'beer off' business known as 'Fox House'. Holes continued to own both pubs until at least the 1950s. Whilst the brewery has been demolished and a private house 'The Old Brewery' occupies the site, the old brewery offices are still standing. The Jug & Glass is still open and is a popular community local, which serves up to three real ales.

Mallet & Chisel   *Hillside*

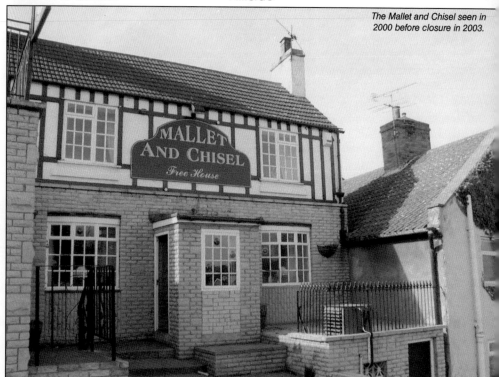

The Mallet and Chisel seen in 2000 before closure in 2003.

First listed as a beerhouse, and known as the Mallet & Tool, this was another former Worksop & Retford Brewery outlet. The building is believed to date back to the 16th century, although the beerhouse business only commenced in the 1850s. It was one of the last beerhouses in the area and did not gain a full licence until 1967. This popular and thriving freehouse on Hillside closed suddenly, and without consultation, in August 2003. It never re-opened, and in summer 2004 Bolsover Council granted planning permission for conversion to a residential property, despite objections from local residents and Chesterfield CAMRA.

The use of the name 'Mallet and Chisel' was probably a reference to the tools used by a stone mason – maybe an earlier landlord had links with this profession.

Portland Arms   *Belph*

This pub at Belph closed in the early 20th century. Belph itself was owned by the Duke of Portland, and most of the residents in the 19th century were his employees. The Portland Arms was first listed in 1852 and its licence lapsed in 1908, when the licensee (R Rawson) died. It is now a private house called, appropriately, 'Portland Cottage'.

Royal Oak   *Bakestone Moor*

Found at Bakestone Moor, originally known as Baxton Moor, the Royal Oak was first listed in 1868 as a beerhouse. The most recent change of brewery ownership was enforced on it in July 1999 when Wards Brewery of Sheffield was closed, and its tenanted pub estate was bought by Pubmaster.

Past and Present

HAVE THEY ALWAYS BEEN KNOWN AS PUBS?

The oldest terms for licensed premises are 'alehouses', 'inns' and 'taverns', as evidenced by a document entitled: 'A list of Alehowsis, Innys, and Taverns in Derbyshire in the Year 1577', which was a survey overseen by Sir Frances Leek.

In general terms:

- Alehouses were the most basic and mainly sold beer. They were often rural.
- Taverns were bigger, found in towns and as well as beer, also sold wines and maybe food. Merchants would meet in a tavern to undertake business.
- Inns, similar to taverns but also offer accommodation.

Taverns had their origin from the Roman occupation ('taberna') and inns were also a Roman concept.

Beerhouses were introduced by the Beerhouse Act of 1830, with the aim of encouraging a return to beer drinking away from gin ('mothers' ruin'). The act made it possible for any householder to retail beer from their premises, upon payment of two guineas for an excise licence.

Pigot's Trade Directory, 1835 refers to Taverns, Public Houses and 'Retailers of Beer'. The latter were beerhouses, whereas the former two were fully licensed, so could also sell wines and spirits.

The last beerhouse licences disappeared in the 1960s/1970s and 99% of all outlets are now licensed to sell beer, wins and spirits. The exceptions are a handful of cider houses in the south west of England, which can only sell cider.

The terms public houses ('pubs') and inn tend to be used interchangeably. In theory, an outlet is only called an inn if it offers accommodation. Use of the term tavern died out in the 19th century, and public house ('pub') is the more common term now.

The George, Marsh Lane part-deomlished in 2003.
"If you don't use it, you lose it"

CLOSED PUBS

Many of the local pub closures in the last 10 or so years are recorded in this sad section although please note that this list is by no means exhaustive. The date given is the approximate date of closure, where known.

Pub	Date	Notes
Barrow, Barrow Hill	2003	
Black-a-Moor, Troway	2008	Fate awaited *SINCE REOPENED*
Bootmakers, Spinkhill	1998	Bought by Catholic Church
Bulls Head, Eyam	-	
Butchers Arms, Marsh Lane	2008	*SINCE REOPENED*
Carr Vale Hotel	1995	Now a shop
Corner Flag, New Whittington	2007	
Corner House, Chesterfield	2000	Now shop units
Cromwells, Bolsover	1995	Licence not renewed
Crown, Wensley	1991/92	
Dale Inn, Whitwell Common	1994	
Duke of Wellington, Shirland	1997	Converted into flats
Feathers (Old), Chesterfield	2003	
Furnace Inn, Birdholme	2002	
Gate Inn, Mastin Moor	2005	Demolished
George, Marsh Lane	2002	Demolished May 2003
Golden Ball, Renishaw	1999	Chinese Restaurant from May 2001
Hare & Hounds/Harlequin, Palterton	1995	Licence not renewed
Hathersage Inn	2001	
Hide-Away, Stretton	1997	Converted to a house
Holly Bush, Grangemill.	2004	
Holmewood Hotel	2000/01	
Jolly Farmer, Holmewood	2008	
Lion & Lamb, Eckington	2001	Demolished March 2008
Lords Arms, Temple Normanton	1998	Licence not renewed
Mallet & Chisel, Whitwell	2003	Now a house
Manor, Northedge	1995	Sold at auction as a dwelling
New Napoleon, Ogston	2007	Now a house
Poplar, Old Whittington	2003	Now a house
Pig of Lead, Bonsall	1995	Now a house
Prince of Wales, Brimington	2007	Demolished February 2008.
Queens Head, Clay Cross	2003	Now a Cantonese restaurant
Queens Park Hotel, Chesterfield	1997	Demolished
Racecourse Tavern, Whittington Moor	2003	Converted to offices early 2005.
Railway, Netherthorpe Staveley	2003	Converted to a house
Robin Hood, Holmesfield	2002	Now houses
Royal Oak, Mastin Moor	2000	Demolished summer 2003
Saint Inn, Chesterfield	1994	Now church social centre
Shoulder of Mutton, Clay Cross	2000	Now an Indian restaurant
Square & Compass, Chesterfield	2001	Now a coffee bar
Station Hotel, Arkwright Town	1995	Licence not renewed
Terminus, Brampton	2002	Demolished to make way for flats
Travellers Rest, Barlow	1992	Licence not renewed
Travellers Rest, Shuttlewood	2005	Demolished for housing
Three Fishes, Stretton	2000	Now a children's nursery
Waterloo, Lower Pilsley	2003	
White Hart, Tupton	2001	
White Hart, Walton	1999	Demolished June 2003
White Hart, Eckington	1999	Converted to flats 2002
Williamthorpe Hotel, Holmewood	2002	
Willows (ex Crabtree), Matlock	2003/4	
Yellow Lion, Apperknowle	2003	Now a house